# Disability Awareness — Do it right!

## YOUR ALL-IN-ONE HOW-TO GUIDE

### Tips, techniques & handouts for a successful Awareness Day

*from the
Ragged Edge Online
community*

*Mary Johnson, Editor*

The Advocado Press
LOUISVILLE, KY

Disability Awareness – Do It Right!

Published by The Advocado Press, Inc., P.O. Box 145, Louisville, KY 40201
www.advocadopress.org

FIRST EDITION

LIBRARY OF CONGRESS CATALOGING-IN-PUBLICATION DATA

Disability awareness - do it right! : your all-in-one how-to guide : tips, techniques & handouts for a successful awareness day from the Ragged edge online community / Mary Johnson, editor. -- 1st ed.
p. cm.
ISBN-13: 978-0-9721189-1-0
1. People with disabilities--Public opinion. 2. Discrimination against people with disabilities. 3. Disability awareness. 4. Disability awareness--Problems, exercises, etc. 5. Disability Awareness Day--Handbooks, manuals, etc. I. Johnson, Mary- II. Ragged edge online.

HV1568.D5675 2006
362.4'045--dc22
2006025807

# Table of contents

**Part 2: Planning and carrying out a successful Awareness Day**

# Introduction

**Workers pair off, two by two. One puts on goggles coated with Vaseline to simulate a vision problem. Another gets into a wheelchair. His partner straps his feet tightly against the leg rests. She uses more Velcro straps to hold his arms against the armrests, to simulate paralysis.**

**"Stations" are set up around the gymnasium. Each is staffed by a student who helps participants "try on" a specific disability. At one, a man puts his dominant arm into a cloth sling which is then tied closely to his body. He will simulate not having an arm. At another, a man is given clean, smooth pebbles to put in his mouth to simulate the speech impairment of someone with cerebral palsy.**

Simulation exercises — activities in which participants get into wheelchairs, tie on blindfolds, stuff earplugs into their ears to "simulate" having a disability — have become a popular "Awareness Day" event. Schools, public agencies, non-profit organizations all conduct simulation exercises.

Although they are popular, these kinds of activities have come under criticism in recent years from people involved in the disability rights movement. And a number of professors who teach disability studies courses in our colleges and universities have serious reservations about them as well.

"Disability simulations do nothing but reinforce negative stereotypes about persons with disabilities," wrote disability activist Valerie Brew-Parrish in the March/April 1997 issue of Ragged Edge magazine. "Jumping in a wheelchair for a few minutes, wearing a blindfold, and stuffing cotton in one's ears does not make a person understand life with a disability."

This handbook is designed to help you understand the disability rights movement's criticism of simulation exercises, and to plan Awareness Day activities that avoid those problems.

The chapters in Part 1 of this handbook offer a short primer on the kinds of problems disabled people face in our society, and their causes. It also discusses the most common problems organizers run into with simulation role-playing. And it will help you understand criticisms of the activity — so that you can decide if simulation exercises are a good choice for your awareness event.

Part 2 offers details on planning and carrying out successful Awareness Day events free from the problems that concern activists. We offer specific how-tos, from setting a goal and objectives, to preparing your Awareness Day organizer and disabled escorts with the background they need, to strategies for ensuring "attitude change" on the part of your non-disabled participants (which this handbook calls "allies"). Chapters give details on how to conduct 6 specific types of activities, how to handle follow-up discussion and ensure ongoing activism, and offer advice on marketing and media.

In the Appendices, you'll find resources and articles to use with your Awareness Day participants.

## About the terminology in this book

The language used to refer to people who have disabilities has been changing for quite a while, and it continues to change. This handbook's language will follow the principles used by activists in the U.S. disability rights movement. When we introduce a word or term for the first time, often we'll take a moment to explain just why we're using that term.

In this introduction we've already used a few terms that might not be ones you use regularly. "People with disabilities" is a phrase that came into use in the 1980s. In 1990, the federal civil rights law known as the Americans with Disabilities Act used similar wording. Such phrases put the "person first." However, in this book you'll find us more often using the term "disabled person" or "disabled people." Many disability studies scholars prefer using "disabled person." They consider individuals to be disabled as a result of society's discrimination.

Like most disability rights activists, we do not use the terms "handicapped" or "challenged." And instead of able-bodied, we use non-disabled. To learn more about these and other terms, turn to the Language Guidelines at the end of Appendix A.

# Part 1:
# Becoming aware

# Chapter 1
# Awareness and prejudice

In the spring of 2006, FX Networks aired a 6-part reality TV show, "Black.White." The premise was simple: two families would trade skin color and racial characteristics, "passing" for people of the other race, living together and sharing their experiences.

The idea of transforming oneself in order to pass as a member of another race — either to gain access to a community normally closed to them or simply "to see what it's like" — was not a new one. In his groundbreaking 1961 book *Black Like Me*, white author John Howard Griffin reported on his undercover experiment as a black man in the racist U.S. of the 1950s. The book was widely read and discussed as the 1960s civil rights movement was getting underway.

Assuming an identity as a member of another group isn't limited to passing for black, or vice-versa. Fourteen years earlier, Laura Hobson's 1947 novel, *Gentleman's Agreement*, which told the story of a Gentile posing as a Jew, also enjoyed a wide readership. More recently, columnist Norah Vincent went undercover as a man for her 2006 book *Self-Made Man: One Woman's Journey into Manhood and Back*. (Publicity for the book at http://www.norahvincent.net /SelfMadeMan.htm says it "will transform the way we think about what it means to be a man.")

The goal of any exercise like this, those doing it almost always say, is to "change attitudes." And that's what "Black.White." producer R. J. Cutler wanted as well. "Racism is prevalent, and white America and black America are two different places," he told reporters. "The only way they're really going to become one is if white people can find a way to see the world through the eyes of black people — and vice versa. Race is the central defining issue in America today. It's the foundation of everything."

Rapper/artist Ice Cube, another of the show's producers, called "Black.White." a way to "expose the subtleties of racism, the layers of racism."

For six weeks, the African-American Sparks family of Atlanta (Brian, Renee and son Nick) and the Caucasian Wurgel family (Carmen, daughter Rose and Carmen's boyfriend Bruno Marcotulli) talked to each other, and what they said was filmed for the TV series. They'd traded skin color, thanks to a team of Hollywood makeup artists, and shared a home in the suburbs of Los Angeles. Cutler believed it crucial for the families to live together. "A lot of discussion [will] be generated in each family coaching the other family on what it is to be white or to be black, and to pass or behave or act as white or black," he said.

But despite all the good intentions, "Black.White." came in for a lot of criticism. "We're always being asked, 'Won't it upset people?'" Cutler told reporters. Not intentionally, he said. "The idea is to make people talk."

The two families talked, too. But did attitudes change?

Bruno Marcotulli continually accused Brian Sparks of seeing racism where none was intended. Sparks responded that the white Marcotulli simply didn't understand the subtle nature of racism. After the experiment ended, Marcotulli continued to say racism was exaggerated by many blacks, who, he felt, needed more positive attitudes.

Even though Marcotulli had "played black" for six weeks, Sparks said, the white man had simply been unable to understand what it was like to live as a black man in America. Bruno Marcotulli didn't see the racism — didn't want to see it, refused to see it, Sparks said.

"Look, I've been black for nearly 41 years, and like all black people I know the difference when a white person has had a bad day and when they are treating me badly because I'm black," Sparks told Marcotulli when the two were interviewed on a talk show later.

"It took awhile for Marcotulli to come to grips with what was going on and what he was seeing," Ice Cube would say to reporters.

Putting on blackface, in Sparks' opinion, hadn't taught the white Marcotulli much at all. "You don't get it — with or without the makeup," he told him heatedly.

"Just because you have on a black face doesn't mean you understand" racial oppression, Ice Cube said.

**A number of viewers and racism experts criticized "Black.White." USAToday's Robert Bianco put it most succinctly, though. "Black. White. is based on two false premises, one more pernicious than the other," he said.**

1. **"that you can understand someone of a different race simply by putting on makeup," and**

2. **"that you need that kind of understanding in order to treat people as the law and morality require."**

When organizers stage disability simulations as part of an Awareness Day event, they may run into the same kinds of criticisms "Black.White." encountered. The criticisms may take them completely by surprise. It may seem that critics are "making a mountain out of a molehill," because, after the event everything seems fine. Those who participate say they've "learned." People thank you. They talk about how "positive" the exercises were.

Still, the critics may insist that simulation events send hidden messages — the wrong kinds of messages.

To see if the criticisms have substance requires a refresher course in prejudice.

## The nature of prejudice: an overview

Many of us who stage Awareness Days would say that people are not really prejudiced against disabled people; it's just that they don't understand them. People don't have enough information about disabilities, we say. If people have negative attitudes toward disabled people, learning more will be "a positive experience" for them.

But you don't have to be mean-spirited to be prejudiced. That's something social scientists have known ever since they began studying the phenomenon.

Perfectly nice people can be prejudiced, can be bigots. And the bigotry can hide in plain sight as well.

Gordon Allport, the Harvard-trained psychologist and theorist whose 1954 book *The Nature of Prejudice* became a bible for those working on desegregation issues in the 1950s, was one of the first to point out that "nice people" can hold prejudices.

A prejudiced or bigoted person is sometimes described as holding a set of negative views about a certain group of individuals — in effect, "pre-judging" them, based not on actual experience with those individuals but on some internal set of beliefs about them. ("Prejudice is an antipathy based on faulty and inflexible generalization. It may be felt or expressed. It may be directed toward a group or an individual of that group," wrote Gordon Allport in *The Nature of Prejudice*.)

Where those beliefs come from is a topic that has been much debated by psychologists. No one has ever thoroughly explained it.

But virtually all sociologists today agree that society plays a role in prejudice.

There are permissible and impermissible prejudices in society. Impermissible prejudices are prejudices that most in society recognize as such. They are out in the open, and are no longer condoned.

Racism, although it certainly exists, is an impermissible prejudice. That is, most people now know that it's wrong to be racist.

## Permissible prejudices

Psychoanalyst Nancy Chodorow describes "permissible prejudices" as ones that nobody really recognizes as prejudice, what Chodorow says are "taken-for-granted assumptions of basically well meaning people." You might also hear them called "rational" prejudices.

"Prejudices are always historical and cultural," she points out. "From the point of view of the person who holds a prejudice, it is not one. "

Chodorow says prejudice against gay people is a currently "permissible prejudice." People still use "fag" and "homo" to put down people they dislike or consider odd or effeminate. Jokes about being gay are still regular elements of television and movies. "In our society, we pass laws against gay marriage, say that discrimination against gays is okay, and people from ordinary citizens through the Senate rail against homosexuality. Homophobia on the individual level usually also has a conscious rationalization.... A man explains his gay bashing as a reaction to having had a pass made at him. A senator invokes the Bible." Many people today believe there is "something special about or innate to homosexuality" that makes it different, and that therefore their attitudes about gays simply make sense," says Chodorow.

People who hold a permissible prejudice assume their beliefs are not in fact prejudice — that they're simply the truth. And because there's no real pressure from society for them to think any differently, they don't have any reason to question their beliefs. After all, nobody's really criticizing them for it.

Racism "among otherwise enlightened white people" in the 1950s was at the time a permissible prejudice.

## How does one lessen prejudice?

People working in civil rights in the 1950s read Allport's book and became convinced that if only white people could be educated, they would come to see their attitudes about blacks were wrong. They'd come to see their prejudiced views for what they were, and they'd change.

Allport believed prejudice was reduced by intergroup contact — but, he said (and it was a really important "but"), this would work only if certain conditions were met:

☛ The two groups have equal status.

☛ The two groups are working towards common goals based on co-operation.

☛ Intergroup contact is both frequent and of a duration that allows meaningful relationships to develop.

☛ Social and institutional support is given.

If these conditions were not met, he said, contact might actually increase prejudice.

This became known as Allport's "contact hypothesis" for reducing prejudice, and it spurred many racial desegregation efforts. Having black and white children attend school together would go a long way toward ending prejudice, people thought.

The "contact hypothesis" is also behind the efforts to have kids with disabilities attend school alongside their non-disabled peers, in the same classes. Both R. J. Cutler and Ice Cube, who produced the "Black.White." reality series, seemed to be pinning their hopes on the "contact hypothesis" as well.

Social psychologist Thomas Pettigrew was a student of Allport, yet Pettigrew didn't think that merely having individuals mix with and educate other individuals would do much to change prejudice. He concluded that schools, public agencies, churches, civic organizations all "institutionalized" prejudice. That is, these institutions behaved in a way towards blacks that was not only prejudiced but that essentially ratified prejudiced behavior as the norm. Until these institutions' actions were changed, he believed, little else could be accomplished in terms of lessening racism.

Once institutions — schools, workplaces, neighborhoods —routinely encouraged optimal black-white contact, racial attitudes would begin to improve, he said.

White Southerners were not all mean-spirited people. Many of them did not overtly hate "Negroes." Nonetheless, the social structures of the time created a society in which racism was the order of the day, and people simply conformed to the systems they lived in and thought little about it.

Disability rights attorney Harriet McBryde Johnson says, "When bigotry is part of mainstream culture, it feels like 'the way things are.' My grandfather's generation of white men in the South didn't recognize sexism. They thought women really were magnolia blossoms requiring protection. They didn't recognize racism either. They thought African-Americans really were inherently inferior, suitable to menial work, and that the structures of segregation were for the good of both races. They'd say it wasn't prejudice, but the way things are. This is where we are with disability today."

Until Pettigrew published his theories, people trying to work on prejudice had not paid much attention to social structures. It didn't seem to occur to them that institutions — social structures — went a long way toward justifying the persistence of racial prejudice.

In the 1950s South, segregation was believed to be important to the smooth working of society. "Negroes" were believed to be naturally inferior to whites. "Jim Crow" laws, said Southern whites, were necessary.

Today these are considered racist beliefs; we say they have no basis in reality. Holding such racist beliefs, society now says, places African-Americans in an inferior position in society and denies them equal opportunity.

But many well-meaning people in the 1950s believed those things, and felt Jim Crow laws were necessary and right.

What changed things?

**Activism changed things. Attitudes did not change until structural changes in society were brought about by activists, who held boycotts and sit-ins and marches, and it was these actions, rather than mere education or a change in attitudes, that brought about the end of Jim Crow segregation at lunch counters and in public buses.**

Because of the activism, laws changed. Under pressure from public opinion and from lawsuits, institutions began changing. Society itself began dismantling racism in its institutions.

Watching these battles caused Pettigrew to form his new theories about how prejudice lessens. He became convinced that the real way to change individuals was through social change.

"Education" by itself did not change people, he decided. No; it was structural change — institutional change — that typically preceded attitude change.

Pettigrew's insights turned the conventional wisdom upside down. The conventional wisdom said that "the hearts and minds" of people must first be changed by education and moral persuasion before society would change. Pettigrew discovered that, in fact, it was exactly the opposite.

Pettigrew talked about what he learned from watching the sit-ins of the early 1960s:

"These sit-ins were really well-organized. The men were dressed in suits and ties, the women in their best dresses, so that the issue was clearly racial and not social class. First the protesters would sit down at the lunch counter, and then they would begin to sing, sometimes God Bless America, sometimes the Star-Spangled Banner.

"The whites couldn't take it. Either they were infuriated at what they saw or they were moved to sympathy. You couldn't be neutral."

The sincerity and seriousness of the protests impressed Pettigrew, but he was most impressed by their focus, he told *Psychology Today* some years later.

"The kids who took part in the sit-ins taught social scientists quite a lot."

If the college kids of the day had stuck to the conventional wisdom, Pettigrew said, "they might not have organized the sit-ins because they would have learned that that wasn't the way to bring about social change — they should first work on the attitudes of white people.

"Fortunately, they knew better, that the way to change society is to change its institutions first."

# Chapter 2
# The prejudice of ableism

Disability studies scholars call disability prejudice "ableism." Most people have either not heard of the word "ableism" or they think it's a joke.

Like "racism," "ableism" is a term meaning prejudice and discrimination — against people who have disabilities. It's the belief that disability in and of itself makes one in some way lesser, less deserving of respect, equal treatment, equality before the law. One Harvard professor defines ableism as "the devaluation of disability" that results in "societal attitudes that uncritically assert that it is better... to walk than to roll, speak than [use] sign [language], read print than read Braille. . . " [Thomas Hehir in the article "Eliminating Ableism in Education, in the Spring 2002 *Harvard Educational Review*].

Ableism is a permissible prejudice: one we don't recognize as any kind of prejudice at all.

For many of us who organize Awareness Days, ableism isn't something we think much about. But an understanding of ableism is crucial to creating an awareness event that truly changes attitudes. This chapter gives an introduction.

Is there really such a thing as disability prejudice? Many people would say "no." "Nobody is against the handicapped," Sen. Tom Harkin said not long after the Americans with Disabilities Act became a federal law in 1990. And most of us think that's true. We certainly think it's true when it comes to our own attitudes and beliefs.

## Personal attitudes

What about jokes about "retards" and "spastics?" Nobody means any harm, right?

What are some of the other beliefs we hold about disabled people? Here are some that people have listed on the Ragged Edge editor's "Edge-Centric" blog:

- ☛ "Disabled" is "disabled" all the way down: if you have one disability, people think you have a lot more. If you are in a chair, you are probably deaf and cognitively disabled, too.

- ☛ On the other hand, people are suspicious of anyone who has more than one disability: a wheelchair user who's legally blind; a deaf woman who has fibromyalgia: "people don't know how to process things when there's more than one disability."

- ☛ Disabled people are angry at the world; they are selfish, too, wanting more than their fair share.

- ☛ Disabled people are dependent upon the government for financial support.

- ☛ Parents are angels for raising their disabled children.

- ☛ Parents who abuse (or murder) their disabled children were driven to it by the disability and should not be condemned.

☞ God sends parents a disabled child because they are so full of love.

☞ What a disabled person lacks in one sense he makes up for in another: the blind have a more developed sense of hearing than the sighted, for instance.

☞ People with disabilities go around suing everyone who makes them angry.

☞ People with disabilities are suffering saints; suffering makes you more spiritual.

☞ Disability means you have sinned and are being punished.

☞ Your disability could be cured if you only had enough faith.

☞ A person — man or woman — who is in an intimate relationship with a disabled man or woman is either a saint or perverted.

☞ If you don't "see" a disability when you look at me, I must not have a disability (that is, I am faking my disability).

☞ If you have a disability, you're incapable of handling your own affairs or living your own life or making your own decisions.

☞ People with disabilities must be protected.

## Try this exercise!

**What are some other stereotypes about disabled people? Make a list. Notice how many of them contradict each other.**

## Society's attitudes

Our public policies and public discussions about disabled people also contain stereotypes.

☞ Pundits make the point that most disabled people don't want to work; they're lazy.

☞ Entertainment giants poke fun at disabled people as scammers and slackers. A Simpsons episode, "King Sized Homer," has Homer Simpson trying a work-from-home scam due to his size (the "Am I Disabled?" book he consults lists "hyper-obesity" and "lumber lung"). A King of the Hill episode finds Hank forced to hire a man on drugs because of the Americans with Disabilities Act.

☞ Some conditions, we say, don't exist at all: repetitive stress injuries and multiple chemical sensitivity are two of the ones that get the most public criticism.

☛ People who claim they're disabled like getting government benefits, commentators insist.

On the other hand,

☛ Disabled people are said to make good workers; they don't mind working at repetitive jobs. You hear this comment about people with mental retardation who work as baggers in the grocery or who work stuffing envelopes or other repetitive tasks.

☛ Disabled people are thought to be inspirational. The Sunday newspaper features a disabled teen who has a smile for everyone she meets. A TV newscast reports on the young veteran who's overcoming his war injury, determined to walk again.

☛ We say, "If I think I've got it bad, all I have to do is think about So-and-So who's confined to a wheelchair! Then I count my blessings!"

We know that disabled people face problems. There are still a lot of buildings that wheelchair users can't get into. Blind people can't go to a public meeting and expect someone to hand them an agenda in Braille. Deaf people can't go to a doctor's office and expect the doctor to be able to talk to them in sign language. But, we say, none of this means anyone is prejudiced against these people. It's just the way things are.

**People say...**

☛ You shouldn't expect a doctor's office to have somebody on staff that can use sign language. It would cost too much. The doctor probably doesn't have any deaf patients anyway.

☛ You can't expect shop owners to remove steps to their front entrances. It would cost too much. "Nobody in a wheelchair ever comes in here, anyway," you'll hear a shop owner say.

☛ You can't expect a public agency to prepare an agenda in Braille just on the off-chance that a blind person might wander in. That would be too much effort. It would cost too much.

☛ And you surely can't expect an agency like a public library to use non-chemical cleaners or to ban patrons from wearing perfumes just on the off-chance that someone who's chemically sensitive might wander in. That would be ridiculous.

☛ If a wheelchair user, or a deaf person, or a blind person, or somebody who reacts badly to the chemicals in perfume happens along, and runs into a problem, it's too bad — but it's nobody's fault. It's not like people are actually bigoted against them.

**We must not think there is anything special about or innate to disability that makes it different — that makes it OK for us to hold the negative feelings we do about people who have disabilities.**

## Unconscious feelings

Prejudice has a lot to do with unconscious feelings and fears, say psychologists.

Contact with a disabled person may remind us unconsciously that our own bodily perfection is an iffy thing, a thing that we can lose in the blink of an eye, were we to contract a disease or have an accident. We may not think any of this consciously. It's all going on unconsciously, where it exerts quite a bit of power over our psyches.

Seeing a disabled person will remind us of all of this stuff churning within us, say psychologists. So without even realizing it, we "project onto" disabled people our negative feelings and beliefs.

We will want to protect ourselves from associating too closely with such people, lest the thing we unconsciously fear — disability — somehow rub off on us, or lest others identify us with that person who has bodily or mental attributes that we want to make sure nobody thinks we have.

But because all this is going on in us entirely below the level of consciousness, we would never think that we were prejudiced against someone with a disability.

Yet we only need look at the reactions of people very much like ourselves who participated in Awareness Day simulations to see that something very much like this is going on.

"Today was kind of scary, especially crossing the road," one university administrator who'd participated in an Awareness Day simulation at Queen's University in Kingston, Ontario told a student reporter

"It was a sobering experience," another administrator agreed. "There is a terrible sense of isolation …we're in these silos individually."

"I briefly felt how it would feel to be wheelchair bound for life. I couldn't keep the tears from my eyes," wrote a student at the end of a disability simulation at a high school. "I felt like I was in a small, dark room," said another. She was grateful at the end of the day that should could remove her blindfold, she added, "because so many people do not have the option of taking off the blindfold."

"That's a natural reaction!" you say. "Of course you'd be upset if you couldn't walk, or see, or hear! Anybody would!"

**The producers of "Black.White." wanted to "expose the subtleties of racism, the layers of racism." When we stage a "day in a wheelchair" event, do we say it's to "expose the subtleties of ableism, the layers of ableism?"**

Robert Fuller, in his book *All Rise*, makes the point that "to create a movement, you need to know both what you're for and what you're against.

> Try to imagine a civil rights movement absent the concept of racism, or a women's movement without the concept of sexism. Until the targets of injustice have a name for what they're suffering, it is difficult to organize a resistance. *In some situations, they*

*may even blame their predicament on themselves and each other,
never achieving the solidarity necessary to compel their tormentors
to stop.* [italics added.]

We'll come back to Fuller's insight a little later on.

Can we see the discrimination that's directed against disabled people?
Disability Activist Cliff Payne says,

> People turned on their televisions at night and saw people in their
> Sunday best being attacked by dogs and pushed down the street
> with fire hoses. People could see the discrimination.
>
>   But when you can't get voting materials in an accessible format,
> or when you can't get into a store to shop, few people in society
> see that. They don't get to see the effects of being discriminated
> against. The social costs of people being unable to participate in
> the essential civic duty of voting, the economic effects on society
> and the personal effects to the man of not being able to shop are
> not visible to the majority society.

Payne's point is that the discrimination is in a sense hidden. But that's only
part of the explanation. The other part is that people don't believe anyone is
doing any of this deliberately to hurt disabled people. "Nobody is against the
handicapped," as Sen. Harkin said.

In other words: people think there's no *animus* against disabled people.

Disability rights attorney Steve Gold puts it more simply: "The fact that a person using a wheelchair cannot get up two steps into a store, or cannot get on a
bus, or that movies aren't captioned, is not looked at as a violation of that person's civil rights."

Thomas Pettigrew's analysis of racial prejudice showed that the way to change
society's attitudes was to change the behavior of its institutions, and disability
activist Joe Harcz echoes that wisdom.

"The 1964 Civil Rights Act could not change people's hearts and minds, but it
could allow and enforce access to things like lunch counters, bathrooms, trans-
port, the ballot box. The 1964 Civil Rights Act could not keep a Southern bigot
from hating black folks in his/her heart. It could and did, however, when
enforced, guarantee that a black person could sit at the same lunch counter and
get the same sandwich for the same buck as any sort of white bigot or any person
for that matter.

"Equality of opportunity is enforceable, measurable and the first order of business in any sort of civil rights effort." He continues,

> We have hundreds of thousands of disabled people held in institu-
> tions to this day. And this attitude stuff ain't doing them a bit of
> good until they get the hell out of the prisons that they are cur-
> rently in.
>
> Attitudes do not get changed in a vacuum. They don't get

changed by debate. They get changed in the integrated life of day-to-day community involvement.

If we aren't in schools because they aren't accessible, if we're not in places of public accommodation, if we're not in public buildings, then this won't happen.

You can't change attitudes towards race if segregation is still prevalent and widely accepted. And you can't change people's attitudes toward us if we are continually excluded from the mainstream through a variety of barriers.

"I have no argument with trying to change perceptions and attitudes," he insists. "But I will concentrate on changes in actions — especially in design and implementation."

Abolitionist leader Frederick Douglass said something very much like this in the 1800s. He wrote in his autobiography that "the way to break down an unreasonable custom is to contradict it in practice."

**Or, in other words, to change the attitude, you have to change the behavior. That's what civil rights activists in the Sixties discovered, and it's still true.**

# Chapter 3
# 'Everything you learned is wrong':
## unintended lessons of disability simulations

Why have an Awareness Day, anyway? "To raise awareness, of course!" Yes, and if we prod a little more, we get this response, too: "To change attitudes!"

Does a disability simulation activity, that staple of so many Awareness Days, change attitudes?

Remember the criticisms of the reality TV series "Black.White."?

Many disability activists say disability simulations don't do what organizers intend for them to do. They say they don't really foster understanding. Some say they are actually harmful.

Complaints about disability simulations cluster around three points. The first two echo Robert Bianco's criticism about of "Black.White." He said that the series was "based on two false premises.": "that you can understand someone of a different race simply by putting on makeup, and that you need that kind of understanding in order to treat people as the law and morality require."

The third criticism is that simulations produce unintended consequences.

"[E]ven carefully designed tools that measure intended learning may neglect to measure unintended learning," wrote disability scholars Sheryl Burgstahler and Tanis Doe ("Disability-related Simulations: If, When, and How to Use Them in Professional Development" online at http://staff.washington.edu/sherylb/RDSissue022004.html)

This third point is related to the specific nature of disability prejudice, which we looked at in the previous chapter.

This chapter looks at some common "unintended consequences" of disability simulation activities. To do this, we start by looking at 3 typical Awareness Day events: For each, let's try to determine what the organizers hoped to accomplish.

### 1. "Learn what it's like, see how it feels."

A flyer announcing a simulation exercise for "home care" workers tells participants that the point of the activity is to let workers "know what it's like" for the people they will be "caring for." Nurses attending a continuing education workshop are put into wheelchair "to see how it feels." An instruction booklet provided by a public agency to help Awareness Day organizers explains: the point of putting people in wheelchairs and tying on blindfolds is to "show the physical challenges that persons with disabilities face every day."

### 2. "Shoes of A Dyslexic"

A private school on the West Coast hosts a "Put Yourself in the Shoes of a Dyslexic" Day. Many parents attend.

There are six "learning stations." At one, participants put on heavy gloves and try to button a shirt. At another, they put plugs in their ears. At another, there are earphones to slip on. The earphones fill their heads with static noise. Their job is to try to hear what the person staffing the booth is saying to them.

At the next booth in the row, the task is to put on goggles smeared with Vaseline and try to read the newspaper articles provided at the booth.

"The stations are designed to be stressful," says a press release from the school's development office. "Participants may become fatigued and even emotional."

The school believes the simulation event "leads to greater empathy and understanding of the problems" disabled people face, and "gives insights into working effectively with these individuals."

### 3. Architects' education

Architects are invited to a seminar on accessible design; part of the seminar involves putting on blindfolds or getting into wheelchairs and trying to navigate through the building. They're told they're doing this so they will learn exactly why it's necessary to make a building accessible to wheelchair users and blind people, and what specific things need to be done to accomplish that.

While the third activity actually has a specific objective — the architects know their task is to learn what it's like to get through a building using a wheelchair or without sight — it's hard to tell what the goal is in either of the first two events. Perhaps it has something to do with "understanding": "Knowing what it feels like to be a disabled person," as one of the organizers put it.

It seems probable that this organizer, with her vague response, has not truly "deconstructed" the activity in order to assess its likely effect. Perhaps she, like many organizers of such events, has not had the tools which this handbook provides in order to do so effectively.

In order to think through disability simulations like these, it's important, first of all, that we understand that participants can easily come away having learned lessons that we never intended to teach.

## Focusing on impairment

"Uncomfortable. Irritable. And a little grumpy. Those were my initial feelings," wrote Lance Crossley of the *Halliburton Echo* after participating in a disability simulation like the first one described above.

The workshop, Crossley wrote, was "an exercise in empathy.... Participants are asked to burden themselves with various accessories that emulate dysfunctions that come with aging and then to carry out a number of simple tasks with their newly impaired selves. Those who are...suffering don't have the luxury of shedding their disguise when the lesson's over."

Crossley writes,

At one of the first stations we are told to do up two buttons on a dress shirt. Seems simple enough, but the shirt is white, as are the buttons, and my cataracts don't allow me to discern the contrast. Even when I do locate them, the lack of sensation in my hands makes it difficult to put the button through the slit....

"Not to be able to see well has got to be the most difficult thing," one of the participants tells Crossley.

"Most disability-related simulations are designed to result in negative feelings," wrote Burgstahler and Doe.

By disabling participants and simulating problematic experiences, given their new limitations,... participants learn how difficult it is to maneuver a wheelchair, how frustrating it is to be unable to hear or read, how frightening it is to be visually impaired, or how impossible it is to participate in activities without the use of their hands.

They focus on what people with disabilities cannot do rather than on what they could do with appropriate access, technology, or skill.

Burgstahler and Doe highlight the most common complaint about disability simulations — that they produce negative feelings. Carol Marfisi, of Temple University's Institute on Disabilities, says, "Imagining yourself having a particular disability only serves to reinforce one's anxiety and sympathy towards people with disabilities."

Much of this problem has to do with the fact that what participants are focusing on are the individual impairments rather than the prejudice and discrimination. And the way most simulations are set up almost guarantees this outcome. Carolyn Tyjewski, a doctoral student in Cultural Studies at the University of California/Davis has a term for this: she calls it "individuation of impairment" — academic language meaning it focuses exclusively on the actual "impairment."

But, you may ask, what's wrong with that?

Disability movement experts insist that it's not realistic. It's not accurate. ("Those who take the time to have a conversation with me get to know 'the inside' me, the normal high school student," says Washington's Daman Wandke, who has cerebral palsy. "We need to look beyond stereotypes... to create a more equal society.") And focusing on the impairment means we don't focus on the ableism. The focus is on "how individual bodies function in an ableist society," says one scholar, "as if this is the central question. "The focus, he says, "should be on the ableist society itself."

Simulations like these "aren't designed to address disability as anything other than a personal issue, a personal experience," says Tyjewski. As such, they don't address the real issue, the "larger social problem."

Simulations give a skewed understanding of living with impairment. "Implicit in the exercise is a sense of loss," is how James Overboe, in the Department of Sociology at Wilfrid Laurier University, puts it. Yet because simulation is such a realistic learning method — it's something the participant actually *does*, it's not just intellectual but visceral, emotional learning as well — it's very hard to convince someone who's been through one of these exercises that they in fact did not get anything close to an a true picture of what it's really like to be disabled.

"An able-bodied person could never begin to imagine my life," says Marfisi. For starters, they'd have no ability to sort out the positive experiences from the negative ones, she says. The things Marfisi experiences as a disabled person, she points out, "have been filtered through my particular situation and personality construct."

Awareness takes time. When John Howard Griffin assumed the role of a black man in the pre-integration South, he did it for months. Norah Vincent infiltrated men's institutions as an undercover man for over 18 months. The producers of "Black.White." kept the two families in their roles and interacting with each other for more than 6 weeks. Awareness Day simulations, on the other hand, generally last for no more than a few hours.

Yet even this short amount of time seems to convince participants that they can now pontificate about what it's like to be blind, or deaf, or use a wheelchair. (We'll look at this Know-It-All Effect in a few pages.)

Impairment is personal. An individual's experience of any particular impairment is unique to them. Tyjewski names two other disability scholars, who, like herself, would be labeled "partially blind." "But we do not see the same way," she says. "Our experiences of 'blindness' are very different from one another on a personal level." This isn't simply because the actual disabilities are different; it's also due to age, class, and other differences, she adds.

Learning about impairment, therefore, gets an Awareness Day participant only an idiosyncratic — and probably skewed — impression of "what it's like to be (fill-in-the-blank)." And it misses the boat altogether when it comes to what organizers are probably hoping for but clueless about: having participants learn how to make things better for disabled people.

Because they focus on individual impairment, simulations don't address the "heart of the disability experience," says Tyjewski.

If, however, she gets together with those other partially-sighted scholars "and we discuss some of the things that we've experienced in terms of discrimination, prejudice and oppression, we would have some very similar experiences," says Tyjewski.

"We may not decide to handle these experiences in the same ways, but we would share common ground — *with regard to these experiences.*

"I share that common ground with other people with very different disabilities," she says; "people who are wheelchair users and who have other impairments."

What Tyjewski is talking about here is the Common Disability Experience — the experience that simulations by themselves simply cannot capture, no matter how well planned they are.

**To recap: simulations almost always by design focus on the impairment, rather than on the social experience of disability, the common disability experience.**

Sadly, that's actually one of the draws of simulations, says Chapman University political science prof Art Blaser (see his article on page 109.) "One of the reasons disability simulations are so popular is that they take the focus off oppression and social change, and instead put the focus on simplistic solutions: "be nice."

Participants in simulation exercises may tell you that the experience was a great one. But the "hidden learning" that's going on, too — learning that the participant isn't even consciously aware of — may not be so great. It may have simply taught them how sad, how frustrating, how awful it is to be disabled.

Most organizers don't know how to set up a simulation exercise that teaches anything other than what one "can't do." So most simulations end up "teaching" that the problem is the body, with its impairments. Even if that's not what the organizer intended, that's what participants learned. That's what we mean by "unintended learning" or "unintended consequences."

**Two aspects of this unintended learning come in for criticism again and again. We'll call them the "Newbie Gimp Syndrome" and the "Know-It-All Effect."**

## The Newbie Gimp Syndrome

When participants simulate being blind without having any of the skills a real blind person has acquired, skills like how to navigate with a white cane or how to work as a team with your very own guide dog (who's learned to partner with you during an intensive training program), they understandably feel awful after the experience. People simulate paraplegia by trying to use a clunky junker "airport-type" wheelchair (a "piece-of-shit wheelchair" in Carolyn Tyjewski's words) but without the stronger shoulder muscles which someone who's really a paraplegic has built up. They don't get to use a motorized wheelchair, which has become the vehicle of choice for many people with mobility impairments. If they were to get into a motorized chair, they'd not know how to operate it. Like driving any vehicle, it takes some practice. You don't know the little tricks of how to turn wheels to get over bumps; you're not aware, as someone who's used a chair for years knows, that most sidewalks slope toward the street, and how to keep the chair going straight under such conditions. And so on.

"Those airport type clunkers — got no suspension system to speak of... make the whole 'simulation' thing a living nightmare!" said one activist.

But many organizers would say that's just what they hope for! They want participants to experience that emotional whammy of suddenly not being able to reach things on the top shelf, not being able to open doors, of not being able to find your way about, of not being able to communicate, of having people ignore you when you speak.

Activists will tell you, though, that there's no guarantee that those feelings of being helpless, being shunned will jell instantly into an understanding that much of this stuff is the unfair treatment and lack of access that are the hallmarks of ableism. People are just as likely — more likely, say those who know — to get stuck in that Newbie Gimp Syndrome of simply hating everything about "being disabled" — with no emotional tools to sort it all out.

"When one is actually disabled, the mental, emotional, physical, and spiritual processes all eventually come together in that person," says Marfisi. But that takes time. Remember what Brian Sparks says to Bruno Marcotulli after the 6-week "Black.White." reality show is over? "I've been black for nearly 41 years, and like all black people I know the difference when a white person has had a bad day and when they are treating me badly because I'm black," he's told him. "You don't get it — with or without the makeup." The response to a 3-hour simulation is generally just "relief that they don't have to actually be disabled like this," says another scholar.

The Newbie Gimp Syndrome means you have no guarantee that the lesson you want to each will be the lesson participants learn. There's a better than likely chance, actually, that participants will simply come away with a feeling of just "how awful it all is."

## The Know-It-All Effect

Disabled people often report that non-disabled people feel free to explain to them what they're doing wrong with their lives, as if the disabled person's own living out of the disability experience conferred no particular expertise in the matter. The non-disabled person seems to believe she can help teach the disabled person how to handle their emotions better, how to "overcome their handicap," how to "be positive in spite of" the disability and in general how to live a better life.

It's a little like Bruno Marcotulli in "Black.White." lecturing Brian Sparks on what is and what isn't racism, or like the line in My Fair Lady: "Why can't a woman be more like a man?" But while we recognize (and maybe even laugh about) the Know-It-All Effect when it comes to members of other groups, we often don't recognize when we're doing it to a disabled person, or that there's anything particularly wrong with it.

In his classic book *Stigma: Notes on the Management of Spoiled Identity*, sociologist Erving Goffman wrote that society regarded someone with a disability as a "Failed Normal." That self-explanatory term shows why someone who's not disabled, who's "normal," will naturally figure they have both the authority and the duty to show the disabled person what they need to do to get "back on their feet," as we say — as close to normal as they're capable of doing.

Simulations simply accelerate the Know-It-All Effect in anyone prone to it. Someone who's gone around in a wheelchair for a few hours thinks they can now lecture a wheelchair user in how to handle a situation in which they find other people talking not to them but to the able-bodied person they're with. Someone who's stuffed cotton in his ears for a day feels no compunction telling his aunt, who's losing her hearing due to age, what it "feels like"; he knows, of course, because he participated in a Hearing Awareness Day event. Someone in the grip of the Know-It-All Effect feels free to provide solutions to disabled people who may simply not have figured out the things he figured out during the hours he was simulating that particular impairment.

Prof. Lennard Davis is describing the Know-It-All Effect when he writes in the introduction to *A Disability Studies Reader* that

> When it comes to disability, "normal" people are quite willing to volunteer solutions, present anecdotes, recall from a vast array of film instances they take for fact. No one would dare make such a leap into Heideggerian philosophy for example or the Art of the Renaissance. But disability seems so obvious — a missing limb, blindness, deafness. What could be simpler to understand? One simply has to imagine the loss of the limb, the absent sense, and one is halfway there. Just the addition of a liberal dose of sympathy and pity along with a generous acceptance of ramps and voice-synthesized computers allows for the average person to speak with knowledge on the subject.

Non-disabled people learn from movies and soap operas that their role is to cheer up the disabled person or counsel her, which in reality turns out to be a kind of instructing — telling a disabled person how to feel and react: "you should be grateful… " "you just need to try harder… " "you should think about the positive things in your life… " Most people who've been disabled for any time at all will at some point be on the receiving end of such instruction.

## Not all impairments can be simulated

Only certain kinds of impairments lend themselves easily to a participant exercise. Many kinds of disabilities — cognitive impairments, behavioral impairment, "mental illness" — are ones that can't be simulated easily or at all. Impairments that are easy to mimic — orthopedic impairments, vision loss, hearing loss — are, not coincidentally, the least stigmatized in society.

And it is stigma, far more than impairment, which defines the core of the disability experience — and the thing that it would most profit participants to learn about. (We'll read about stigma in Chapter 5.)

The overarching problem with using disability simulations is that they suggest you need that kind of make-believe experience in order to convince you to "treat people as the law and morality require," to use the phrase from *USAToday*'s Robert Bianco, who was referring to racism.

## The enduring allure of disability simulations

Still, despite the many problematic outcomes of simulations, people just seem to love doing things like tying on those blindfolds, poking in those earplugs or plopping themselves into wheelchairs to "see what it's like."

Could there be a little voyeurism involved? Beth Ferri thinks so. Ferri, an associate professor in the Disability Studies program at Syracuse University, got a hint of this when she happened upon two different disability simulation exercises in progress — one while walking at a state park, another at a social agency.

In both cases, the people organizing the activity walked behind the students, who were blindfolded and paired up with a sighted student who was assigned to be their "eyes." In both cases, the organizers trailing the group were "having a lot of fun" watching the "spectacle," laughing at the problems the ersatz blind participants were running into.

It likely never occurred to either of the organizers that the behavior was in any way "disrespectful."

But now think about the idea of learning about sexism, racism or homophobia by mimicking a member of one of those groups. It seems faintly wrong, doesn't it? Perhaps it seems that we'd be "disrespecting" blacks, or women or gays to do such a thing. We'd probably fear that doing so publicly would cause an uproar.

But the idea of a disability simulation being criticized by disability movement activists usually doesn't occur to us. We'd think twice about trying to put on blackface — we'd figure there'd be an outcry from civil rights activists or some African-American group. But we just don't expect that sort of thing to happen when the topic is disability.

So we feel free to use simulation activities. They seem like clever things to do. A break in the routine way of learning.

There's likely another reason as well, directly related to the point about "individuation of impairment" which we discussed earlier in this chapter, on page 17: When we set out to learn about gays or racial minorities, what we typically have in mind to learn about is how they're treated in society. Often we want to learn about the injustices so we can work to do something about them.

But when most of us think about "disability", what pops into our heads are simply images of specific impairments: Blindness. Paralysis. Deafness. ( Perhaps we think of someone we know who has such an impairment.) We may believe doing a simulation exercise is truly the only real way to learn what we think we need to know. We may really think disability can't be understood any other way.

What this says is that what we think we need to know about is the "impairment." But that's not a part of the disability problem that we are even particularly capable of doing anything about.

What we are capable of doing something about, though, is the discrimination disabled people endure. **Through collective action, we really can reduce ableism. Participants can use their energies to improve the lives of disabled people here and now, by working to remove discrimination, which shows itself in exclusion via lack of access.**

Awareness exercises can empower us to start that work, if they teach us not about the "individuation of impairment" but the Common Disability Experience. That is, if the exercises and activities have been designed the right way; if they've been designed to do that.

That's what Part 2 of this book is all about.

# Chapter 4:
# Learning to recognize ableism

In the last chapter, we learned that disability activists say that simulations, because they focus on individual impairment, don't give participants an accurate picture of what it's like to be disabled. An accurate picture, say activists, would show that most of the problems disabled people encounter are either brought on by or exacerbated by society.

The following story from disability activist Susan Fitzmaurice helps us see what this means:

> I cannot walk without pain. So my house is set up so that I do not have to walk long distances without a place to sit. When I go outside my house I use a scooter. If there are ramps and wide enough doorways, I can use my scooter with ease. My pain never disappears, but my environment can protect me from unnecessary pain and allow me the opportunity to not be forced to walk.
>
> I am also severely hard of hearing. My son knows to look at me when he talks. We listen to music and the TV loud. He knows that if a sound is low I will not hear it, so he makes sure I know what I need to know about it. Outside our home I struggle with people covering their faces when they talk, talking facing away from me, talking quietly, with environmental sounds being too low for me to hear, and so on.
>
> My son has Down syndrome. Inside our house it is understood that he needs to be independent and make choices. Every opportunity is afforded him to be credited with the ability to make good and bad choices (short of ones that would cause him harm because of an inability to understand the consequences). Outside of our house he is constantly being shortchanged. People are not inclined to take the time to understand his inarticulate speech or his use of less-adult language to describe adult feelings. His speech and language ability do not change when we leave the house, but the social environment he interacts with does.
>
> Our disabilities do not disappear, but the disabling features of them can be eliminated or reduced.

Fitzmaurice gives a good description of how society ("outside our house") causes problems for a disabled person — problems that make being disabled worse than simply having the impairment. People "aren't inclined to take time to understand" her son's inarticulate speech. People cover their faces when they talk, and then she can't understand them. If there are no ramps where she needs to go, she can't use her scooter, and walking causes her pain. All these are things that are done by other people.

These things could be changed, though. People could do things differently. And if they did, life would be better for Fitzmaurice and her son, even though their impairments themselves didn't change at all.

But, beyond that: **These changes would help many other people whose impairments may be similar to or very different from Fitzmaurice's or her son's. The changes would help everyone.**

It's important that we start thinking this way whenever we think about a disabled person's situation or "problem." Then we can separate out what part of the problem is due to the impairment, and what part is due to situations created by society or by other individuals. And then it's an easy jump to thinking about the role we can play in changing the "society" part.

This chapter will help us learn to recognize ableism in society.

## A matter of focus

What is our goal for an Awareness Day? What do we want participants to learn?

**If we focus on the impairment, they learn:**

☛ how hard it is to open a jar when one has arthritis.

☛ how cataracts and glaucoma make it impossible to read small print.

☛ how hard it is to understand written instructions when one has dyslexia.

☛ how it's often impossible to open doors or get up and down curbs when one uses a wheelchair.

**If we focus on the "disablement" caused by ableism, they learn:**

☛ how hard it is to use everyday things when manufacturers don't use "universal design" principles.

☛ how hard it is to read when those who produce printed materials use tiny print.

☛ how professors discriminate when they refuse to provide instructions in alternative formats, as they're required to do by law.

☛ how hard it is to get into a store when the owner hasn't provided the ramps and lighter doors now required by law.

The examples above are a little bit like that common perception puzzle: You're given a piece of paper with the black silhouettes of two people kissing. Or is it really just a picture of a white vase in the center of a black background? It depends entirely on your perception, doesn't it?

## A lack of recognition

Ableism isn't part of most people's vocabulary the way "racism" and "sexism" are. It's not something you hear people talking about on TV, like you heard about "racism" when "Black.White." was airing. A search of news stories over the last two years turned up thousands of references each to "sexism," "racism," "homophobia" and "ageism" in the nation's news media. Fewer than two dozen used the term "ableism."

Because people have no name for the phenomenon, it often doesn't occur to them that such a thing even exists. There is, after all, a perfectly good explanation for why disabled people have problems: it's because their bodies have something wrong with them. They have a disease. They've had an injury. It seems perfectly clear to most folks that the person's own impairment is the problem.

Let's come back to what Robert Fuller said on page 12. The point he was making was that until people have a name for an injustice, they don't recognize it as one. And they blame not the injustice but its victims.

Most people simply see the "disability problem" as the impairment. (They're seeing the white vase in the middle of the paper, not the two black faces kissing.) Because of this, most public activity on behalf of people who have disabilities is some sort of activity to find a way to treat or cure impairment. Even activities that don't focus directly on cure or treatment are usually aimed at helping disabled people become as close to "normal" as they can be.

Put another way: It's clear that people think the problem is the impairment because most public activities "on behalf of the disabled" are related to helping them lessen their impairment, rather than working to end discrimination, as we do when we create programs to help gays or racial minorities or women.

☛ Think of the "race for the cure" events sponsored by disease charities. Breast cancer charities use events like this.

☛ Think of the telethons, especially the big one, the Jerry Lewis Labor Day Telethon. Think of the donation jars at supermarket checkout counters. Think of the lapel pins and stickers they sell to raise money for a "fight to find the cure."

☛ Think of Christopher Reeve's unflagging battle to walk again. Think of how he spoke out publicly to raise money to find a cure for spinal cord injury. Think of actor Michael J. Fox's fundraising to find a cure for Parkinson's.

☛ Think of the Ronald McDonald Houses, the Make A Wish organizations.

☛ Think of the public service announcements asking listeners to support diabetes treatment centers, to find a cure for cystic fibrosis, to give to the Mother's March to end birth defects.

This is what most of us think of when we think about public awareness efforts related to "disability."

All of these very public efforts are charity efforts, though, not civil rights or social change activism. They say the problem is the specific impairment.

It's no wonder we've internalized that message.

Now try to name a single disability group whose fight for rights or access comes close to any of these national charity efforts in terms of public attention.

## Try this exercise!

**Make two columns on a sheet of paper. Put "treatment/research for cure" as the heading in the left-hand column. Put "activism for access/equal rights" as the heading in the right-hand column.**

**Now list all of the news articles, public service announcements, ads, posters, special events and other publicity you can think of from the past 12 months, putting them under one heading or another.**

**Which heading has more items under it? Why is that?**

People are mostly unaware of the existence of any strong national collective disability voice. Because that's the case, there seems to be no "official story" about the disability discrimination experience, no common articulation.

Instead, there are many seemingly equal and competing public stories about disability:

- Disability is a tragedy and disabled people need cures (Jerry Lewis's and Christopher Reeve's message).

- Disabled people want society to bend over backwards to give them special privileges (talk show commentators and pundits).

- Disability groups hurt American business by suing to enforce expensive access regulations (judges, attorneys, business groups).

- Parents of disabled children have unrealistic ideas, and demand "inclusion", draining much-needed resources away from the normal child (school boards, parent-teacher groups).

- Disabled men and women who set their sights on once again becoming productive members of society are getting rehabbed and returning to normal (injured Iraq war veterans).

- Poor disabled people need your help and charity so they can "get back on their feet" (groups like Goodwill, Salvation Army).

It's a national cacophony — a lot of different competing noises, making it almost impossible to hear any one noise clearly.

Each of these "national narratives" about disability in a sense cancels out the others, so that most people simply don't know where to turn for "awareness." Which "awareness"? Which narrative will you select from?

## Public images

Say the words "civil rights movement," and what comes to mind? Television images of firehoses and police dogs set upon civil rights marchers in the early days of the civil rights movement. George Wallace at the schoolhouse door, forbidding integration. Rosa Parks refusing to give up her seat in the front of the bus.

Say the words "gay rights": people think of the Stonewall riots. They think of the murder of Matthew Shepard. They think of "gay marriage."

Say the words "women's movement." "Bra-burning" springs to mind. Women demonstrating to protect abortion rights.

These images may not conform to actual history. And you may find some of the images distasteful, or contrary to your own political beliefs. But that's not the point. The point is that we do, as a culture, share a set of common images for other movements.

## Try this exercise!

**What images does the public have for "disability rights"?
What images for "ableism"?**

Once we begin recognizing the role that society plays in "disabling" people, we can get to work truly making things better for disabled people. It's not like trying to find a cure, or pioneer a new therapy or treatment. We don't need vast amounts of scientific knowledge. No; disability prejudice and discrimination can definitely be lessened as a result of collective social action. No new drug needs to be discovered. No cure needs to be found. No new surgical procedure needs to be perfected. Solutions, in fact, already exist. We have models already, from other civil rights movements. All that needs to happen is for society — both institutions and individuals — to change behavior.

Another way we might say this:

> **We're already equipped and able to fight ableism, if we only learn to recognize it.**

# Chapter 5
# Ableism's personal toll

The dearth of common images for disability rights and ableism — this lack of focus — affects individual disabled people as well.

This is important to understand. Because of how ableism is often "internalized," not all people who have impairments — people we might consider to be disabled — will want or know how to assist in carrying out the kind of Awareness Day activities we discuss in Part 2 of this handbook. (In Chapter 7, we give organizers suggestions on how to find disability activists who can help with Awareness Days.)

We may, in fact, not know any disabled individuals or any disability groups who could speak to us on "awareness." Even if we know someone who has an obvious disability, we may wonder if they would feel embarrassed if we drew attention to it. Enough people who have disabilities insist that "I don't consider myself 'disabled'" (see Appendix D) to make this a realistic concern. Should I ask John at my church, who uses a wheelchair, when he doesn't appear to be involved in any disability rights group or activity? Maybe it would embarrass him. Maybe he doesn't want attention drawn to being disabled.

The conventional wisdom has always said that disability is medical — and medical matters are supposed to be private and personal. One isn't supposed to draw attention to them. (People who talk about disability generally talk about their own impairment and their troubles with it and are labeled "whiners." "They're not working very hard to overcome the disability," we say.)

The idea of a common disability experience doesn't much occur to anyone outside the organized disability rights movement. Because that idea is not widely accepted or even understood, because the term "ableism" is so little known, people who have disabilities mostly learn to go it alone, to try to "get back to normal" as much as they can the best way they can.

Relatively few people who have impairments really have any desire to "come out as a disabled person." What would be the point? They may not know if there is a disability community in their town. They would not know how to find one even if they had heard one existed. And what would a disability community do for them, anyway? If they do know about one, they may feel it is too activist, filing lawsuits and such, or they may think it's a dippy do-nothing group. Neither appeals. Their goal is not to become like other disabled people. Indeed, just the opposite: for most disabled people, the goal is to return to "normal", as far from other disabled people as possible.

## 'Passing'

If you can't actually become normal through cure or treatment, you may be able to "pass" as normal. And so "passing" becomes a goal for many disabled people.

Because so many people who have disabilities have worked to "pass" — or, even if visibly disabled, to distance themselves from "disability" — any given disabled person is likely to be a poor choice to educate a group on awareness. Which of the competing narratives about disability do they personally ascribe to? Are they Tiny Tims?

A majority of people who have disabilities still see their problems as caused primarily by their impairment. It's not that they don't run into bigotry, prejudice and discrimination. They likely encounter it daily. When a spinal cord injured guy with this outlook can't find a parking spot his lift-equipped van can park in (because a non-disabled person is illegally parking in one of the reserved spots); when he can't get into a building because of a step; when he can't use the restroom at the bar because it's not big enough to get into in a wheelchair, rather than viewing the problem as one caused by the bar owner, who is breaking access laws, he simply focuses on the fact that he's in that wheelchair. If only there were a cure, and he could walk, his problems would disappear! That's how he thinks.

This is a description of a man stuck in the "medical model." And many many people with disabilities view things this way.

Although a disability movement is growing, vast numbers of people who have disabilities still know little about this movement, and personally do not know any disability activists themselves. And far too many wheelchair users today still blame their predicament on themselves. That is, when they encounter barriers, they become angry that they're in a wheelchair. It's because they're in a wheelchair that they have problems. That's how they think of it. They don't think of it as a problem caused by lawbreakers who are not providing access as federal law requires — or, if they do realize that laws are being broken, they don't know what to do about it. The idea of banding together with other paraplegics to demand enforcement of access laws simply doesn't occur to many disabled people. It might be a good idea, they think, but they would have no idea how to go about it, or where to find others who would want to do it with them. And it doesn't seem right to file lawsuits. People don't like those who file lawsuits.

In a public climate in which there is no one set of images that tells us what "disability rights" means, what "ableism" means, the idea of figuring everything out for yourself, by putting on that blindfold or getting into that wheelchair, seems to many of us to come down to the most sensible way to sort it all out. That seems to parallel what real disabled people are doing in their own lives. They deal with their impairment by themselves. They don't let themselves think too much about things like bigotry and oppression. They try to be "positive" about their situation, as society expects them to be. They try to pass, to the extent that they can.

"I'm a 32-year-old woman, disabled since birth, and until recently I have been firmly in the closet," wrote Candice Lee, who was born with what she describes as "a congenital defect of the lower spine." Lee's essay, "From 'Passing' to 'Coming Out'" was printed in the Sept./Oct. 2003 issue of Ragged Edge magazine and is online at http://www.raggededgemagazine.com/0903/0903ft2.html

"I have been living in the non-disabled world all my life," she wrote. "I am a full time professional. I have been married eight years to a non-disabled person.

"In most of the situations I encounter, I am the only person present with a disability. All the key disability rights issues — work, housing, medical care — have left me unscathed, because of my fortunate ability to work full time, to put a roof over my own head, to purchase health insurance."

Lee, in short, seems to have been able to "pass" fairly well. But, like most disabled people in her situation, there's something that messes things up:

She writes, "here are these braces. This limp. This ostomy appliance. These stares in the supermarket. All remind me that, while I live among the non-disabled, I remain on the margins. I remain Other."

What Lee is talking about here is stigma. In his book *Stigma: Notes on the Management of Spoiled Identify*, sociologist Erving Goffman explains that the Greeks "originated the term stigma to refer to bodily signs designed to expose something unusual and bad about" the person. (The Greeks actually branded the person with a mark, called a "stigma.") In his book, Goffman uses the term "stigma" to mean any attribute, physical or mental, "that is deeply discrediting." Note that the "discrediting" is being done by others; by society.

"As I age have I begun to realize that I have spent all my life among the non-disabled trying to measure up," Lee wrote.

> If I am smart enough, maybe They won't notice my limp. If I am pretty enough, maybe They will accept me anyway. If I am accomplished enough, maybe They won't mind my braces.
>
> There are rules for passing. First, I must come up with a nice, short, palatable, cocktail-party explanation of my disability to set people at ease when they ask. Nothing too scary. And then, I must never mention it again.
>
> I must learn to change my ostomy appliance in less than five minutes standing up in the stall of a public restroom. I must work hard to keep up while walking with others. I must act like I don't mind when they leave me behind. I must arrange my doctor appointments during off hours so I don't appear to be taking too much sick time. And I must never, ever mention the rigors of life in this body. To do otherwise draws Their attention to my otherness.
>
> And They do Their part, too. I can't tell you the number of people who say, "I just don't see you as disabled," or "I had met you three times before I noticed your braces." Most folks just can't reconcile the me they meet with the images of disability generated by the media — the only images they have.

## Seeking the disability community

The late policy analyst and disabilities scholar David Pfeiffer said, "To name a person as 'disabled' is to give them an inferior position. In our society people identified as disabled are second-class, third-class, or even worse-class citizens. We live in a constant state of discrimination. Identifying oneself or another as a 'person with a disability' is an ideological act. There's no other way to describe it."

When people who cannot manage to "pass" say nevertheless that they don't "consider themselves 'disabled'," it means they are also not openly living as a disabled person — by which we mean they are not living their life in a way that acknowledges the role of society in the problems they encounter in their lives. They do not talk about their lives as Susan Fitzmaurice does, whose comments began this chapter.

There's a middle stage between "passing" and "living openly as a disabled person" — a stage in which you may admit to yourself that what you're up against is prejudice and discrimination, but you're not yet ready to acknowledge it publicly — because to do so gains you so little in a society without a vibrant disability rights movement. State your feelings openly, and you may very well find yourself alone with your beliefs, offered little understanding from your non-disabled community, which only wants you to "pass for normal."

People who find themselves in this emotional state are seeking the disability community, even if they don't realize it.

Pfeiffer said,

> Being a "person with a disability" is a damning thing and not everyone can or wants to be damned. I do not want to be damned. I do not care about being "disabled" in the sense of impaired — everyone is or will be impaired. Hopefully some day being impaired will not mean being damned, but it does today in our society. But knowing firsthand (and sometimes crying from the pain) what it means to be disabled/damned, I can not condemn anyone who renounces the label "disabled." I want to hug them and acknowledge their pain, but they (almost always) can not even think of such a possibility.

> They go their way with my blessing.

We go back now to the second part of what Robert Fuller said on page 12

> Until the targets of injustice have a name for what they're suffering, it is difficult to organize a resistance. *In some situations, they may even blame their predicament on themselves and each other, never achieving the solidarity necessary to compel their tormentors to stop.*

Now go back and read that second part in italics again:

**In some situations, they may even blame their predicament on themselves and each other, never achieving the solidarity necessary to compel their tormentors to stop.**

The wheelchair user whose day has been spent encountering one after another after another illegal violations of access laws has no name for the oppression he's experiencing. He has never heard the word "ableism" other than as a joke. He has no idea how to organize a resistance.

This chapter has offered just the briefest glimpse into the workings of ableism in the lives of individuals, by showing us some of the typical kinds of emotional responses and reactions many people have to living as a disabled person.

Almost all of us will either acquire impairments and become disabled at some time, or we will be close to someone who does, so this information may be useful for us in the future as well.

This chapter and the one preceding it help us begin to understand the pervasive but mostly unrecognized damage ableism causes in the lives of individuals and in our society. There are suggestions for further reading in the Appendix as well.

Part 2 of this handbook suggests ways we can begin to raise awareness in order to reduce the damage caused by ableism.

**Part 2:**
**Planning and carrying out**
**a successful Awareness Day**

# Introduction

What characterizes a successful Awareness Day event? Is it one in which participants have learned what it feels like to stare through grease-smeared goggles, to try to hear through earplugs, to try to button shirts with fingers taped up? Or is it one in which participants learn from disabled people how to become allies in the work to create a more equitable, more accessible society?

"However they may be constructed, we are never, ever going to give anyone the full spectrum of the 'disabled experience', which is subjective and relative anyway," says Lawrence Carter-Long of the Disabilities Network of New York City. "But simulations can help people get more familiar with our issues."

> Do we limit our opportunities to confront bias against disability if we, on principle, reject simulations? Or can they be constructed in ways that work to our advantage?

> If simulations have any value, it's that they can help demystify interactions with real, live disabled folk and, just as importantly, provide a unique opportunity for non-disabled participants (perhaps unwittingly) to confront their own assumptions about our lives.

> Of course, it would largely depend on the construction of the event and subsequent debriefing.

> But the exercise itself is merely a vehicle; a means to an end — or possibly a beginning.

Disability simulations can serve as a means to an end, but so can many other kinds of awareness activities. Part 2 of this handbook offers a way to structure Awareness Days that have a real chance of changing things for the better for disabled people. But we will likely need to throw out the old planning guides we've used in years past and start afresh with a new plan.

And a plan is essential.

Most Awareness Day planning revolves around the day's simulation events. Do we have enough wheelchairs and earplugs? Do we have enough volunteers to staff the "stations"?

This manual is different. It focuses on how to plan for increased understanding of ableism on the part of participants. It shows exactly how to ensure what kind of learning takes place — and how to avoid the "hidden curriculum" pitfall we discussed in Chapter 3.

To do all this, we must look at the roles of those involved in Awareness Days

1. The **organizer**;

2. The disabled **escorts** who will work with the organizer,

3. The **discussion facilitators**, and

4. the non-disabled participants in the event, whom we will call **allies**.

We need to have our calendars handy, because we'll be looking at a months-long process of preparation.

Chapter 7 discusses roles and tasks. Chapters 8 and 9 offer many kinds of activities and tactics to ensure your Awareness Day makes a lasting impression and hopefully a lasting change in the "awareness" of your non-disabled "target audience." Chapter 10 gives you a detailed timeline to follow, and Chapter 11 helps you decide what kind of media outreach you'll need to do.

We suggest reading this manual and starting your planning a full year before your next Awareness event. But even if your Awareness Day is coming up within just a few weeks, this manual's tips and tactics can help you put on a very good event quickly. More important, it will show you how to make next year's event wonderful.

# Chapter 6
# What's your goal? What's your objective?

The very first task in our planning process is to define a goal. Ideally this should be done right after your last Awareness Day event. But certainly it needs to be done 6 to 9 months before your next one.

Many groups don't think overly hard about this part of the event. After all, isn't it obvious that the goal is to "raise awareness?" Or to "let people see what it's like to be disabled"?

If you've read the Chapters in Part 1, you know that this is not the best goal to set. You've learned that the goal of any awareness event should be "to lessen ableism in our community."

That's a very broad goal, of course, but certainly no broader than to "raise awareness." We'll have a more focused objective.

How is "lessening ableism" different from "raising awareness" or "letting people see what it's like to be disabled"? The exercise in Chapter 4 is designed to help you learn this distinction.

In Chapter 3, we read about the simulation for "home care workers" which aimed to "show the physical challenges that persons with disabilities face every day." We read about the West Coast school which hosts a "Put Yourself in the Shoes of a Dyslexic" Day, which it says "gives insights into working effectively with these individuals." We learned about the seminar for architects on accessible design, where they've been told their exercise in traveling through a building using a wheelchair or blindfolded will allow them to learn exactly why it's necessary to make a building accessible, and what specific things need to be done to do that.

The problem with most Awareness Days is that organizers did not think through their goal very carefully — or they simply are not aware of ableism. Organizers focused on impairment rather than ableism as the problem.

Let's look at the following goals which a group might set:

☛ to learn how it feels to be unable to hear

☛ to have participants experience the difficulties that come with arthritis

☛ to experience what it's like to be in a wheelchair

These goals all focus on impairment. Groups promoting these kinds of events typically say that their goal is simply to "raise awareness."

On the other hand, a goal of reducing ableism will ensure that the "awareness" that's raised is an awareness of ableism. Ableism, as we've learned, is the devaluation of disability that results in societal attitudes that uncritically assert that it is better to walk than to roll, speak than [use] sign [language], read print than read Braille, and so on."

In Chapter 1 we learned that social psychologists and civil rights activists both came to the conclusion that when institutions changed, people's attitudes changed, rather than the other way around. Keeping that in mind, let's look at some...

## Goals aimed at reducing ableism:

☞ to learn how ableism affects people with paralysis on a college campus in order to see that it's lessened

☞ to have participants experience the kinds of ableism people with arthritis might encounter

☞ to find out about ableism affects someone who can't hear well

Events built around these kinds of goals will have activities that look quite different from the standard simulation stations. The first goal might lead to an event in which each participant is first given an assignment to walk over a designated section of campus, and, much like one does in a scavenger hunt, "collect" places and things that the participant believes would pose a barrier to a person with either paraplegia or quadriplegia. The second half of the event would pair the participant with a wheelchair using escort; they'd retrace the route to see where the disabled person actually does encounter barriers. They would discuss the difference between things that do and that don't pose barriers, the role of other people in opening doors, what it's like to have to ask for doors to be opened if you have little upper body function, and what happens when no one is around. After that, a post-activity discussion session would have participants pool what they learned from their activity, make a list of which barriers exist, and, finally, to ensure that participants learn how to work to lessen ableism, come up with an plan to force the college to remove the barriers.

An event designed to let participants learn about how ableism affects people with hearing loss will focus on things in the community — in the built environment — that cause problems for people with hearing loss. Allies will learn how deaf and hard-of-hearing activists locally and nationally are taking action to get these things changed.

Other activities which groups with goals for reducing ableism have come up with include the following kinds of exercises:

☞ Allies get into wheelchairs and try to catch a city bus or take a taxi to a meeting.

☞ Allies get into wheelchairs and go shopping for clothes (and find the aisles too narrow and the dressing rooms too small for wheelchairs; the cashier's counters too high).

☞ Allies put on a blindfold and try to use the Internet.

☞ Allies insert earplugs and then try to take a spelling test, with the test words given out by a "teacher" in the front of "class."

## What's your objective?

You've defined a goal. Now what's your objective?

An objective is more focused, more immediate, more specific than a goal. A goal is broad, and relates to values. An objective is a here-and-now thing to get done. It's task-oriented, and has a deadline. The most successful Awareness Days have not only a goal but an objective as well.

The Fresno, Calif. ADA Advisory Committee's objective was specific: They wanted to get the city's 15 public officials to see precisely the kinds of problems Fresno's disabled residents ran into when they tried to navigate around the city. (See "Official Awareness" by Ed Eames in Appendix E.)

Think about some objectives you might set for your Awareness Day. Keeping in mind that the goal is to reduce prejudice and discrimination, and that activism works better than mere "education" in achieving this goal, set an objective that relates to your organization, group or community — one which actually has a chance to reduce ableism.

For discussion purposes, we've created three imaginary groups. Each is thinking about hosting an Awareness Day:

**Help and Hope for the Handicapped, Inc.**, known in the community as "3H", has a 75-year history of raising money through telethons and appeals to help local disabled children ("crippled children," they were called when the organization was new). Its well-known programs include a brace shop, a children's hospital wing funded by the group; a summer camp. Its new Director of Volunteer Training took part in a disability simulation exercise in another state and thinks a similar simulation would be a fun event for training new program volunteers.

**Podunk Community College**'s Director of Disabled Student Services has heard colleagues from other community colleges talk about Awareness Days and thinks it would be a good event for PCC as well. She's heard they are popular and that they help students and faculty understand the disabled student population better.

**ABC, the Anti-Barriers Coalition**, is an organization of disabled individuals and a number of local groups (the local chapter of the Paralyzed Veterans of America and the local chapter of the National Federation of the Blind are both members). This 6-year-old organization wants public officials and bureaucrats to get a taste of what it's like to have to use the local paratransit program— and they'd also like the officials to see what it's like to try to get around the central business district when the city has never bothered to provide the curb cuts and ramps to buildings which are required by federal and state law.

## Try this exercise!

**List 3 objectives each group could set to help them toward the goal of reducing ableism.**

## Using your objective to create social change

You've now come up with 3 objectives that each of our imaginary organizations have set to get them to the goal of reducing ableism. Does each objective involve social change?

Individuals by themselves can't do much to change others' ableist beliefs and behavior, so long as those beliefs are accepted by society as "the way things are." To truly reduce prejudice requires that institutions change as well. When institutions themselves start to change their behavior, we find individual's beliefs beginning to change.

So it's important that our Awareness Day objective focus on changing something on an institutional level.

Awareness Days should affect the institutions where they are held. Good Awareness Days do.

Our schools, public agencies, churches, and social service organizations almost all, to one degree or another, retain at least some ableist policies and practices. If our objective takes aim at this, we have a real chance to make lasting change.

The group sponsoring our Awareness Day may say it supports our awareness efforts. But actions speak louder than words. Set an objective that gets your organization (or a community institution) to acknowledge and change its own ableist behavior.

What you set as your Awareness Day objective will depend on your own organization, your escorts' concerns and your target audience.

The Director of Volunteer Training for 3H, Inc., along with activists from ABC who were going to serve as the escorts for her Awareness Event, came up with idea of getting community websites — the official ones of city agencies and the websites of local news outlets — to be accessible to people who use screen readers. 3H volunteers often came from the ranks of the community's "movers and shakers" and many of them had easy access to city officials. They attended the same churches and country clubs, they played golf together, they were invited to the same parties.

ABC's members had been upset for quite a while that they couldn't take care of the simple tasks sighted residents were now doing online — checking property records, filing business license reports and so on. The local public radio station archived many of its community forums and talk shows with local guests, but it was impossible to use unless you could see. ABC members had written letters and threatened to file complaints. But they realized that if allies, who were friends with the city's business and government leaders, insisted the sites become accessible, things would start moving quickly. So that's the objective they came up with.

At Podunk Community College, Awareness Day this year would serve as the starting point of a very specific campaign: to get the administration to install automatic doors at the main entrance to the student center.

Automatic doors weren't required by law, so members of the disabled student union hadn't had much luck with their efforts to date. They felt that if they could get non-disabled students and faculty to unite behind them on the campaign, they've have a much better chance of success.

In each of these cases, the objective

- ☛ was specific, clearly spelling out a problem in the community that had the effect of discriminating against disabled people

- ☛ focused on making a change in the environment and society (rather than making a change in the disabled person, which is typical when disabled people are told they need "training" or "therapy")

- ☛ involved disabled escorts and non-disabled allies working together for the common good.

Gordon Allport (page 7) said that for prejudice to be reduced, members of both groups had to remain in contact ("contact is both frequent and of a duration") so that "meaningful relationships" can develop.

The kinds of activities we list in Chapter 8 are designed to allow participants to be involved with disabled escorts for a minimum of a few hours to a maximum of a day. But the final Awareness Day activity should include a session in which plans are made for the escorts and allies to continue working together to meet their objective.

In Chapter 8, we'll also look at ways to get your organization to support your work.

If your goal is "to reduce ableism," your participants should be guided by disabled people. After all, they're the ones who face ableism. They're the ones who can best educate the participant. And your event must always end with participants and escorts together planning strategies to change things.

At this point you may be thinking to yourself, "This sounds a lot more complicated than the Awareness Days we're used to! This requires participants to not only do an activity, but discuss it later, and then, looks like, come up with some plan for activism. All we really want is for people to have fun!"

In that case, you might want to consider "doing a simulation without simulation" (see page 109). Or you might want to ask yourself: "Why are we having an Awareness Day? For that, after all, is the first job you have to do when you plan an Awareness Day — you must decide why you're doing it. If you're uncomfortable planning an event in which participants have to confront the reality of ableism, you might need to re-think your reasons for holding an Awareness Day.

# Chapter 7
# Organizers, escorts and allies

## The Awareness Day Organizer

The person in charge of the Awareness Day is the organizer. Is that you?

The Awareness Day Organizer has the overall responsibility for seeing that the group sets a goal and decides on a workable objective for the Awareness Day event. She's also the person responsible for getting disabled people to serve as escorts, taking part in the activities and guiding the non-disabled "target audience" (that is, the non-disabled people we are calling "allies").

The organizer brings to her role the knowledge that the ultimate purpose of an Awareness Day is to reduce ableism. She knows that the Awareness Day must educate participants about the prejudice and discrimination that disabled people face — educate them in a way that will excite both disabled and non-disabled participants into wanting to work together to learn about ableism and fight against it in the community.

The Awareness Day Organizer recognizes that, above all, Awareness Days need to serve as part of the work against ableism that needs to go on in every community across the country.

## Preparing the organizer: education

What's the best way for the organizer to prepare to lead an Awareness Day event? By educating herself, learning as much as she can about ableism and about disability rights activism, and about what activist groups are doing to combat ableism nationwide.

That's one of the reasons we suggest allowing 9 months — or more — of preparation time. It takes time to learn a new area — and this is a new area for many people.

More significantly, learning about ableism often requires that we do some unlearning as well.

It's hard to undo a lifetime of thinking about disabled people as having problems — their impairments — which they are working to overcome with the help of things like speech therapy, training, new an improved "treatments" and special programs designed to help them get "better". It's hard to stop thinking in terms of the "medical model" and start to routinely focus on the role society plays in making life difficult for disabled people.

But it's our job to re-educate ourselves so that, when we think of the "problems" disabled people face, we automatically think not of their specific disease or condition, but about an agency's failure to provide access or accommodations like sign language interpreters, scent-free meeting spaces for people with multiple chemical sensitivities, large-print or taped materials, voice-friendly websites, automatic doors.

Of course not all Awareness Day organizers need this education. You may already be deeply involved in disability rights work or disability studies. You may be an activist yourself or part of an activist group which already knows their Awareness Day is an effort to achieve a community change — like the Fresno ADA group on page 38. You will already either explicitly or implicitly have this education.

However, even the most experienced organizer can benefit from refreshing her knowledge — and examining the knowledge she already possesses — to ensure that the event comes off without the unintended consequences of a "hidden curriculum" (Chapter 3).

On the other hand, you may just now be learning about ableism. You may have never heard of that term before reading this book. Reading Part 1, you may have realized with a start that your group actually does focus on the "medical model" and pays almost no attention whatsoever to the effects of prejudice and discrimination when it seeks to educate others about "disability".

If that's the case, reading this manual is the best way to begin educating yourself.

The materials we've listed in Appendices A and D have been selected to give the organizer a "quick start" education. Appendix C's list of books supplements this "instant" education. And there's a list of books for more long-term study.

Websites are one of the best sources for ongoing education. The websites we list in Appendix A — including the Disability Studies, Temple U. blog, Inclusion Daily News, Mouth magazine, the BBC disability website Ouch! and our own Ragged Edge Online — will give you the most benefit if you make it a point to return to them weekly to keep up on events and read the new essays and blog entries that have been posted. A weekly visit will also help you gauge how much your own understanding is growing.

Is your community home to one of the universities that boast full-fledged disability studies programs? (There's a list in Appendix A). That is an excellent place to get a true education in the topics we've discussed in this book. Sign up for a course, audit a course, or find out about special events and programs they offer. Talk to some of the professors or graduate students. Some of these people may also be interested in serving as the volunteer escorts you will need for your awareness event.

If you're not in a community with a university disability studies program, you may still have a disability rights organization in your community. Get to know its members. Go to meetings, sit in on training sessions, get involved in one of their committees. You may find they're a perfect source for the disabled volunteers who will serve as the escorts for your Awareness Day event.

Some kinds of disability organizations are more likely to be sources of escorts than others. "Centers for independent living" (also sometimes called "independent living centers") are organizations that in theory at least are operated by disabled people interested in social change. Unfortunately, this was more true when the "independent living" movement was getting started in the 1970s and 1980s than today. (In fact, even nursing homes may have "independent living" in their names!) The information on page 77 in the Appendix provides more information on locating independent living centers and suggests some web-based reading to do to learn more about these centers and their philosophy.

"Cross-disability" coalitions and groups with "disability rights" in their name are also promising as sources for escorts. Remember, though, that many organizations concerned with disability are really charity or fundraising groups, or groups providing therapy and rehab services (see page 24). Such groups are not likely to be good sources of the kind of escorts you want.

It's important to keep in mind the distinction between organizations that offer "medical model" services and groups doing social change work. Groups like our fictional 3H, Inc. come under the "medical model." There are far more groups in most communities like 3H, Inc. than our fictional ABC group. It should go without saying that these "medical model" groups, which some activists call them "do-gooder" groups, are not the best place to complete your "anti-ableism education!" Try to figure out who they are, and avoid them as a source of education.

Their members, however, may be in the target group you invite to your Awareness Day!

After you've gotten a ways into your self education, your next task is to find the escorts who will work with you on the Awareness Day.

## The disabled 'escort'

"Just hanging out with folk with various impairments, making daily rounds together, is highly revealing," says Alex J. Lubet, a professor of American Studies at the University of Minnesota.

And what gets revealed is often an experience that could never be simulated.

"Going to concerts with people who need accommodations was a real eye-opener," he continues. "Not that I didn't know intellectually that one can buy a ticket for the same price as everyone else and get that ticket early and still get stuck in the worst seat in the house...."

Lubet's experience with the bad concert seat is one that a person involved in a mere disability simulation would likely never encounter. (For a vivid first-person account of this kind of discrimination, read Susan LoTempio's "A Ticket to Bias" in Appendix D.) Bad concert seats, wheelchair lifts which fail to work (or which can't be unlocked because the key's been lost), a sign-language interpreter hired for an event who doesn't, in fact, know American Sign Language — these are the kinds of real-life experiences that disabled people encounter daily. Typical simulation exercises that don't pair up participants with actual disabled people as escorts don't afford allies the opportunity to observe the real-life experiences of real disabled people, which is what you really need to understand the problems disabled people face.

"It takes practice for other people to understand the ways that disability affects my life," writes Cal Montgomery in the essay "A Hard Look at Invisible Disability," which is available in our Appendix D. "Some experience with me, or at least with people who are like me in some way, will give you a much better handle on what I'm going to have trouble with, and why."

Montgomery is autistic. She writes, "As you come to know me, you'll get better at spotting the barriers I face when I want to participate in the life of my community, my society, my world. You'll learn to spot the strobing fluorescents, to catch the verbal constructions that trip me up, to notice when I cannot recognize the people and objects in front of me and the speech and other sounds around me."

This kind of understanding of how an actual person with a disability deals with barriers is something that can't be gained from a disability simulation. It requires a disabled escort.

Having disabled people escort your Awareness Day participants — either by simply talking about experiences or by allowing the participants to "shadow" them in specific activities" — gives a much firmer basis for understanding the kinds of problems that disabled people as a group experience in society.

And it's a sure way to avoid The Newbie Gimp Syndrome, which we talked about earlier — the syndrome that affects the unprepared person newly thrust into an impairment who ends up convinced by the experience of not being able to see or hear that life for people with such impairments is practically — if not literally — a fate worse than death.

And because it avoids The Newbie Gimp Syndrome, it's without question the only real way of ensuring that allies don't get stuck on the impairment, unable to see the ableism because they're still worrying about the impairment.

## Escorts need preparation

But your escorts can't just assume their roles, either, without preparation.

Disabled people, too, have a "responsibility to continually examine the ableism which we have all internalized," says Sharon Lamp, a doctoral student in disability studies at the University of Illinois-Chicago. Ableism "does not magically disappear, even when we commit ourselves to the disability rights movement." What changes — or what should change, she says — "is our ability to recognize ableism within ourselves as well as society."

Having disabled escorts who are aware of this, and who have spent time processing their own reaction to ableism, means your potential allies stand a better shot at being able to examine the societal barriers and bigoted attitudes (ableism) they and their escort run into, and really begin to think about how to undo ableism in society.

Skilled, prepared, competent escorts are crucial to the success of your Awareness Day event. You will not only be introducing allies to disabled people who are completely competent human beings — who, yes, lack sight or hearing, or who lack functioning legs or arms, or who have an "autistic" way of processing information — but who are skilled at giving the ally an understanding how the incidents they experience together are caused or compounded by ableism.

Recall that the producers of the reality series "Black.White." planned for the two families to live together, so that they could educate each other. Remember Gordon Allport's insistence that "intergroup contact is essential for reducing prejudice." Having disabled escorts is essential to any activity in which you want to truly "change attitudes" and educate participants about ableism.

But because non-disabled people make up most any disabled person's immediate community, "it shouldn't be surprising that most, if not all, disabled people have internalized a great deal of ableist thinking," Lamp explains. In Chapter 5 we discussed how people might internalize ableism; people who all their lives have been taught to regard their impairments as the reason for the problems they encounter in their lives, and to brush off or deny the anger they feel at society's prejudice and discrimination. We also made the point that, while disabled individuals are all around us, that many (including ourselves, maybe) work hard to both "pass as non-disabled" ("I don't consider myself 'disabled'") or to distance themselves from activism, from disability activists and other disabled people in general.

These are, obviously, not the people you will ask to serve as escorts, right?

It's easy to think of people you know who have highly visible disabilities as being a natural choice to serve as escorts for the Awareness Day events. But you need to find out, first, about their own attitudes about ableism and disability rights. In disability rights circles, a person who's clearly disabled but who nonetheless wants to distance himself from disabled people and who disparages disability rights is sometimes called a "Tiny Tim" (much like term "Oreo" has been used in the civil rights movement). You don't want Tiny Tims to serve as your Awareness Day escorts.

So it's important to interview would-be escorts. Ask them their views on disability prejudice, discrimination. Ask them about ableism. Do they even know the term? What do they think about the concept? What do they think about disability rights and disability rights activism?

## Locating disabled escorts

If you're fortunate enough to be in a community where there are known activist groups and individuals — or a strong disability studies program at the university — it should be an easier task to find people to serve as escorts. But unfortunately many of us do not live in communities with such resources. Disabled people are often quite isolated, having no real disability community to connect with locally. However, more and more, such people are finding comrades and community on the Internet.

If you have disability groups in your community, they can be a likely source of escorts. Don't assume, however, just because there is such an organization, that its staff or membership are actually "disability activists." (See page 42 for more details on how to find and assess disability organizations.)

If you find disabled people who really want to be involved in your Awareness Day but whom you feel need some more education in disability rights, spend time as a group preparing yourselves.

Start by reading this manual together and discuss resources you found useful (See Appendix A). Do your own "pre-Awareness Day" to ensure you and they share an understanding of the issues.If even these measures don't produce qualified escorts, then abandon plans to do a "simulation" or "real life activity." Do a different kind of Awareness Day. Suggestions for that are on page 109.

## Discussion facilitators

No matter what your objective, no matter what activities you choose to use, real change isn't going to occur unless your participants and your escorts spend time processing the activities they've done.

Discussion sessions should begin and end your Awareness Day, and unless your disabled escorts have a lot of experience and training in how to handle complex emotional discussions, it would be wise to provide someone with this specific kind of training to facilitate discussions.

Should you bring in a professional facilitator?

Good discussion facilitators can help the group explore their feelings in the emotionally charged climate that often surrounds group explorations of prejudice and bigotry, particularly when some in the group feel they're the victims of that prejudice. There are facilitators who are trained to do just this sort of work. They work for organizations, for church groups, and for companies.

If neither you nor your disabled escorts have experience in facilitating this kind of discussion, you should plan to seek out paid or volunteer facilitators for your Awareness Day event.

They, too, will need some advance education — from your disabled escorts.

Most professionals who facilitate diversity training sessions are well-versed in helping groups explore their prejudices around the well-known bigotries — racism, sexism, homophobia. When it comes to ableism, however, it may be a different story. As we discussed in Chapter 2, many well-meaning people who understand racism or homophobia still don't recognize the bigotry in many of their own attitudes and beliefs about disabled people. The facilitators you plan to use may be part of this group.

Therefore, the first "participants" in your Awareness Day may be your facilitators. That is to say, you and your disabled escorts should plan to meet with facilitators well in advance and give them some awareness training as well.

You should meet at least twice, maybe more, to outline the discussions you plan to have with your allies. Use the same agenda and discussion questions with the facilitator as you plan to use with Awareness Day participants. How do your facilitators do in these discussions? What are their feelings about the issues?

"Not everyone is ready to learn or realize their own ableism," Sharon Lamp reminds us. "Not everyone respects the knowledge that comes from lived experiences of disability" that your event's disabled escorts represent. The time to find this out, and to work through any problems, is well before your Awareness Day.

## Allies

In this chapter, we've referred off and on to the group of people you're trying to educate as both "participants" and "allies." They are your target audience.

The term "ally" is popular today in social justice movements and on campuses. It refers to a person who, although not part of the specific "group," is nonetheless supportive of the social justice goals of the group and can assist in bringing about social change. Articles discuss "engaging men as social justice allies in ending violence against women"; white allies working against racism. Straight people can be allies of gays and lesbians; non-disabled people can be allies in the disability rights movement.

Allies have a unique role. By learning about the kinds of prejudice and discrimination that disabled people face, and learning it from disabled activists themselves, these non-disabled people can come to understand the issues disabled people face in a new way, and respond in a new way as well. In the past, non-disabled people have been considered the experts. Medical professionals, rehab professionals have told disabled people how to live. But the disability rights movement says, "we are the real experts on the issues that affect our lives. Learn from us." Allies learn the issues from disability activists. Thus instructed, they can not only support but amplify the work of the disability rights movement.

## Self-awareness

It's popular among social justice activists today to say that the first job of the ally is to become aware of their own role in oppression. When it comes to disability rights, this may be especially true, because as we learned earlier, disability discrimination is quite often an unconscious act — or at any rate an unthinking act. This doesn't mean it's any less harmful, or that disabled people and their allies should accept it. It does mean that there is a lot of work to be done, work that needs many non-disabled allies to be effective.

"Everybody does it." "It's just the way things are." "Nobody means anything by it." In Chapters 4 and 5 we read about the many ways in which disabled people encounter prejudice and discrimination that "nobody means" — the reluctance to provide an accommodation that means the difference between holding a job and not being able to do the job; a failure to ensure access that results in disabled people not being able to attend the theater or go on the company picnic.

It is one thing for a disabled person to call an organization to task over their discriminatory practices that deny access to disabled participants. Too often, such people are dismissed as "whiners and malcontents." But when their voices are joined by those of non-disabled allies also demanding justice, it becomes harder for people who consider themselves to be "right-thinking" to deny that they are, in fact, discriminating by being slow or reluctant to provide accommodation.

This is the ultimate role of the ally: to join their voices and bodies with activists, supporting their work and raising their issues in their own circles where they are known and respected; to "carry the word" and declare that the time for discrimination is past.

In order to take on this role, however, allies must first be educated. They must first confront their own prejudice, and learn how to move beyond it.

Allies, by their willingness to educate themselves about disability prejudice, by their willingness to learn from disabled people what things need to be changed in society, and by their eagerness to work alongside them to see the changes accomplished, give much-needed support to the movement for justice for disabled people — moral support, financial support, and the support of able bodies to do the work that needs to be done.

We've referred to disability rights allies as non-disabled people. And in theory that's accurate — but there's always a "but.... "

### The pain of 'coming out disabled'

"Disability" is a fluid identity in our culture. Many people who actually have one or more conditions that others might think makes them "disabled" in fact truly don't consider themselves disabled. Candice Lee's story on page 29 showed us this.

It's important to be aware that people who do not actually identify as disabled may find "awareness experiences" unexpectedly painful. Although it wasn't your intent at all, such people may feel particularly threatened or violated by the kinds of discussions that can arise during the event or in the after-event processing.

Because "disabled" is an identity that many people are conflicted about (or actually ashamed of), odd and unsettling things can happen if your Awareness Day events are very good — that is, if they are doing they work they've been designed to do, which is force people to examine their beliefs.

One common reaction is a "coming out": a formerly "non-disabled" person announces that they, too, have such and such a disability.

Does this matter? Ordinarily it shouldn't; ordinarily it should be a very good thing. If this person then forms a bond with escorts and makes a decision to work on fighting ableism, it's wonderful.

But such a "coming out" can provoke a different reaction as well: the participant, having announced that they, too, have a disability, may decide that the escorts are "all wrong" about this or that insight. In other words, a Tiny Tim may emerge. In such situations, the newly "out" disabled person may want to be seen as the expert; may want to strongly argue in favor of the medical model; may insist that officials are not prejudiced, even though now, decades after federal law has required it, they've still not installed a ramp into City Hall; may insist that blind people "demanding" accessible websites is outrageous, and so on.

Your event, of course, might provoke the same kinds of reactions from truly non-disabled participants. But when that happens, the disabled escort holds an authoritative edge: after all, the escort who's himself blind and who has actually experienced the frustration of not being able to navigate a website and can talk about this obvious need, and point out how easy it is for a business to "do the right thing," if only they would. But when the "non-disabled person "comes out" as actually being legally blind herself, and says that she doesn't think websites should be "forced to cater to" blind people, then the situation is a bit different, and can become difficult emotionally for all involved. This, of course, is what activists mean when they say a disabled person has "internalized ableist attitudes." It's a common problem, and you should anticipate running into it at some point during your awareness event — unless you've designed a very superficial event that nobody gets very involved in!

Your preparatory sessions with your Discussion Facilitators should include plans for what to do in this eventuality; ways to turn the situation into a "teachable moment."

As difficult and uncomfortable as such "outbursts" seem, they are actually a sign that your event is a successful one. They also give participants an opening to talk about how hard it is to work through the societal attitudes we've all internalized when it comes to how disabled people are expected to behave in society; how they are taught to accept a "second-class citizenship" without complaint.

Remember: change — real, honest change — is almost always a bit painful. This is not the only instance in which you should expect your participants to be a bit uncomfortable. You want them to challenge their assumptions. You want their ideas to change.

The difference between your Awareness Day, which you've designed with the goal of reducing ableism, and someone else's vague "education about disabilities" event is that at yours, the change that occurs has a real chance of making society better for disabled people, as participants begin to realize their own role in propping up ableist beliefs. At that point, you will be on the road to gaining real allies in the fight for accommodation and equal access.

That is why we call your participants "allies." Because one of the effects of a truly successful Awareness Day — one you should plan for — is that the non-disabled participants will become allies of the disability rights movement. That is something you should expect to happen. It's what you should aim for.

## Equal participation

The "Black.White." producers knew that prejudice is only reduced when both groups regard each other as equals, as partners in a common endeavor.

Your event has brought together disabled escorts and non-disabled people. Now they must engage in a common endeavor: First, to learn about the reality of the prejudice and discrimination that makes life as a disabled person difficult, and then to figure out what to do about it.

Prof. Mark Sherry, who at the time of this writing held the Ability Center of Greater Toledo Endowed Chair in Disability Studies at The University of Toledo, stresses just how important it is for non-disabled people wanting to learn about disability issues to do more than just imagine the problems, sticking with only an intellectual understanding. He instructs his non-disabled students to "attend disability community meetings to engage with the politics and dynamics." He then asks them to "critically reflect on the power dynamics they witness" and "to assess the potential for useful political interventions." He then requires his students "to carefully reflect on their own impact — and possible future contribution" to the work of the disability community activists in the area.

It's a very good agenda — one you might want to copy.

# Chapter 8
# Designing Awareness Day activities

"In an imperfect society, within an imperfect framework, on a planet where disability simulations are not likely to disappear anytime soon, is it possible to structure them in ways that enable all who take part to truly confront the prejudices they had coming in, understand each other better on the way out and foster a willingness by all to keep moving forward?" asks Lawrence Carter-Long.

"In nearly two decades of strategic communications and advocacy work, if I have learned one thing, it is this," he continues. "True communication occurs when people speak to each other not from where we wish things were, but rather, from where they are.

"Only when that is understood can we move toward where we'd like to be."

You've gotten yourself up to speed on the thinking of disability rights activists. You've talked with disability activists. You've found a group of activists happy to serve as escorts for your event.

What now?

In Chapter 1, we learned that four conditions need to be met if groups actually hope to reduce prejudice. Go back and read those conditions, on page 7.

Here we've re-worded them slightly:

1. The two groups must see each other as equals.

2. They must start to work together toward common ends, cooperating with each other.

3. They must work with each other closely enough so that "meaningful relationships" can develop.

4. They must have a sense that their work is being supported, either by the organization that brought them together or by the larger institution which they are working to change.

Both the disabled escorts and the non-disabled participants who will become allies must respect each other. Too often, non-disabled people regard disabled people as being less intelligent, less capable, less savvy than they are. Often this is utterly unconscious behavior on the part of the non-disabled person, who has no idea that she's coming off as paternalistic. But most disabled people will pick up on that paternalism instantly.

So how can you and your disabled escorts ensure that participants' unconsciously paternalistic reactions are defused? What can your escorts do, how can they present themselves, in such a way that participants regard them as their equals?

Working together to solve a common problem is the quickest way to defuse paternalism — particularly when the problem is one that the disabled person can solve more quickly or more efficiently than the "newbie" participant.

That's where the second condition comes into play: They must start to work together toward common ends, cooperating with each other. This is why an objective, clearly spelled out for participants, is so important. Go back to page 38 to refresh what you learned about setting objectives.

Once you've set a good objective, ideas for activities will start to flow almost effortlessly. Naturally you'll want to select activities related to your objective, won't you?

Notice we're no longer using the word "simulation."

Your disabled escorts will be paired with your participants, either one-on-one or in small groups with fairly even numbers of escorts and allies. In either case, there's no real need for the non-disabled person to "simulate" or "mimic" a disabled person — not when they have a real, live disabled person at their side whom they can observe and question about what's going on! Just as participants do in work-experience events, they can "shadow" the disabled person as they go about the community.

Shadowing is just one of the activities we'll look at: others are investigation, dramatization, role-playing, audiovisuals and plain old discussion sessions. And we should never forget to have fun!

**Before we start listing ideas for activities, we should stop and remember that
the "activity" is only the middle part of the three equal parts of your event: There's the introductory session — discussion before the activity — and there's the post-event processing, the follow-up discussion where the real learning, and the real change of heart, occurs. All three parts are equally important, and must be part of your planning.**

For the activity itself, it's up to you and your escorts to decide if props like wheelchairs, blindfolds, earplugs, Vaseline-coated goggles will actually be useful learning tools. Remembering the kinds of emotional reactions non-disabled people can have to such simulations, be sure your introduction and follow-up discussions will be thorough enough and open enough to counteract any "hidden learning" effects.

## Here's how our three fictional organizations designed their activities.

**The 3H - ABC Awareness Day partnership** had as its objective to get local websites accessible to people who use screen readers. Escorts from ABC, many of whom were also members of the National Federation of the Blind, came up with this plan:

First, the two most knowledgeable ABC members would make a presentation on problems blind people face because of inaccessible websites. They'd explain what the problems consisted of, and stress how simple it was for web designers to make accessible sites, talking a little bit about the technology and the minimal costs. Participants would get to try the technology for themselves during the activity part of the event.

The presentation, which they wanted to make sure was fairly brief — no more than 20 minutes, they thought — would also touch on problems with e-commerce sites like Target and amazon.com, and would talk about activist efforts — including lawsuits.

Then they'd pair off two by two — sighted with blind — and go to the bank of computers in 3H's computer lab. Two members of ABC who were sighted but, because they were quadriplegic, needed to be able to navigate websites with voice-activation programs, were also going to serve as escorts.

They planned to allow an hour for the activity itself. The entire time might not be spent at a computer; that would be up to each couple. But there'd be enough time for the allies to clearly learn what the problem was all about.

They'd do it this way: The blind escort would start the tour at a fully accessible website. Some of them would use the NFB's site for this. They'd show the volunteer how a blind person could surf the web by listening to the voice and by using combinations of keystrokes. As they navigated, they'd answer questions. Then they'd go to an inaccessible website. As they tried to get instructions on what to do, the sighted ally would see that the site wasn't working. They'd ask questions about problems; the blind escort would answer.

The escort would then suggest that the ally put on the blindfold (or Vaseline-smeared goggles to simulate low-vision), which was provided. With this in place, the ally would be told how to get to an accessible site, and, prompted by the escort, do some web surfing using voice-output and keyboard commands. This would show them that they too would be able to learn to use the web, even if blind — except when websites weren't accessible. The lesson? the problem isn't being blind, because, with practice, you can learn to use voice-output software and keyboard commands. No; the problem is websites that aren't accessible.

The third part of the event would be the follow-up discussion. One thing the ABC escorts were particularly interested in, they said, was hearing how the allies felt about running into websites, while blindfolded, that they should have been able to use, but couldn't. Did this make them frustrated? Was the frustration due to their inability to see? Or was it frustration really anger at the company who hadn't bothered to make the site universally accessible? The escorts really wanted to make sure that people came away from the event firmly convinced that the problem wasn't due to blindness but to faulty design.

"People have gotten the idea that blind people have special needs on the Internet, and I want to dislodge that kind of thinking," said one of the ABC activists. "I think it's really important for the participants to understand how incredibly easy it is for web designers to make a site accessible — and that an accessible site isn't special; it simply works for everybody.

"And to understand, as well, that when they don't do it, that's discrimination, pure and simple."

He was insistent that the allies come to this conclusion on their own, from their own experience at the event. This would make them stronger allies when they began working on their friends in high places to get the community's websites accessible, he said.

The ABCers didn't intend for 3H's Awareness Day to be a one-shot deal. They considered it to be the start of an active group of allies.

**Podunk Community College's Awareness Day Committee** (the organizer and the escorts) structured their 3-part event like this:

Part 1, from 9 to 11, would start off with a discussion of campus access. The escorts thought that participants probably believed their campus was pretty accessible — and they suspected that telling them otherwise would simply sound like complaining or wanting too much. So they thought a "before and after" experience would be a good one.

Rather than telling participants about campus access problems, they wanted participants to tell them. Where did participants think the problems were? They'd go around the room, and anybody who wanted to suggest places they thought caused problems would do so — but only if they were non-disabled participants. The escorts would speak later.

Then the participants would be given pencils and notepads and sent off in small groups to various destinations on campus. Their job? To figure how to get into specific buildings if they could neither walk nor use their arms. They were sent out groups to discourage cheating, they were told. Actually, the escorts didn't care if they cheated or not. They just wanted participants to wander about campus and give some thought to something they'd likely not have ever focused on before.

Participants were to meet in front of the student center at 11:15. There they were paired up with wheelchair users, and everyone went off to lunch — which, of course, was part of the observing and learning as well.

This was as close to a simulation the participants would get. While they were not in wheelchairs themselves, or on crutches, they were each paired with someone who was. Their job was to shadow the disabled person. Watch and learn.

And learn they did.

Although it's not a legal requirement to provide automatic doors, it soon became clear to allies that the lack of automatic doors posed an insurmountable barrier. If no one was there to open the door, the disabled person was simply stuck. They couldn't get in. Maybe they could get out — doors opened outward; that was a legal requirement relating to fire codes, and it seemed it was followed to the letter. If a door could be nudged with a wheelchair, or pushed against with one's body (if one were walking or using crutches) the door could sometimes be forced open. But if the doors were the kind that required a lever be pushed down and held down, they were out of luck.

Lunchtime was a busy time on campus, and generally someone was around to open a door. But the escorts were at pains to discuss this point with the allies, and point out that people weren't always around. They also talked about what it was like to travel around campus knowing that you depended on lucking into someone who could open a door. This seemingly simple problem took on a huge dimension. The lack of automatic doors meant one had to always try to think ahead; to plan trips that would involve someone else, always; to be careful not to be on campus late or on weekends and hope to get into some building — if no one was around, you were stuck.

Participants also saw what it was like to need to use a restroom and not be able to open the heavy door.

The hardest part for the fledgling allies, a number of them said in the discussion session that followed, was the requirement that they stay in the shadows, and not help. "Help" was a natural thing to do, many said.

But the point of the awareness exercise was exactly that, they were told: to understand what it's like to not have help; to not have to seek "help." The problem, participants were told, wasn't the lack of "help" — the problem was having your life controlled, messed up, complicated, by a simple barrier — a barrier that simply didn't have to be.

The discussion session, scheduled to run from 2:00 p.m. to 3:30 p.m., ended up running quite a bit longer as the escorts and allies sat around mapping out the campaign to get the administration to install automatic doors not only in the student center but the library, the 3 dorms and Merritt Hall as well — for starters. Then they planned to press for a campus whose doors all opened automatically. Some of them were working on campaign slogans as the day ended: "We have automatic doors for groceries and luggage! Now we want automatic doors for people!"

## Simulations

Simulations are only one kind of activity. It's interesting, though, they they've emerged as the most popular Disability Awareness Day activity. Might it be true, as Prof. Ferri felt (page 21), that they offer certain voyeuristic possibilities?

Training and awareness events to educate about racism, sexism, homophobia or other forms of prejudice don't use simulations. When was the last time a diversity training session had white participants put on blackface? Or had men pull on wigs and wiggle into skirts and heels?

### Try this exercise!

**Discuss among yourselves why "simulations" aren't done with other kinds of "awareness" training. Then ask yourself why it might be such a popular approach to disability awareness training.**

Our fictional organizations used techniques other than simulations, and we've outlined them below. Shadowing, investigation, dramatization, role-playing, audiovisuals and discussion are time-tested educational techniques that will probably get you closer to your objective than simulation.

## Shadowing

"Shadowing" has been popularized as a technique to give young adults a taste of the job world. A teen spends a day following the worker ("sticking to her like a shadow") observing everything she does, how she does it, when she does it, where she does it. Designed to be a one-on-one activity, it gives the teen a real feel for what a job is like, and gives him a specific individual to talk to, bringing up any questions he has.

In our example above, Podunk Community College's Awareness Day participants were shadowing their disabled escorts as they traveled with them around campus and watched as the escorts tried to get into various buildings.

## Investigation

When 3H's volunteers first watched as the ABC escorts surfed the Internet using voice output software, and then tried to do it themselves, they were investigating. It certainly involved the ally in a participatory activity, but it wasn't simulation.

The first part of Podunk's awareness activity was also an investigation. When allies were sent out in groups to determine how to get into specific buildings, they were investigating.

Investigating is a good activity. Allies can be told to go investigate to figure out how a wheelchair user can get from one destination to another marked on a map. They must mark curb cuts, ramps, doors, obstacles sticking out into the sidewalk. They can do the same to see how a blind person can get from here to there. They can try to take a taxi to a meeting while using a wheelchair or try to go from x to y without using their hands.

Chapman University's Prof. Art Blaser's article on page 109 gives a list of suggestions for investigations.

Investigations work best when the ally — who, after all, is untrained — is given a checklist of things to look for and mark off. It might not occur to them that things like low-hanging signs or flagpoles or hanging flowerpots protruding out over the sidewalk, or signpoles, could pose a real hazard for a blind person unless it's discussed beforehand and listed on their check-off sheet. It might not occur to someone who's walking that a 1-inch lip at the bottom of a ramp would make the ramp useless for someone who had no way to get their wheelchair up over the bump. And, sadly, it's not all that unusual to find a ramp that, at its top, has a small step!

Investigations work best if you plan, as PCC disability activists did, for a two-part activity in which allies are first sent out to investigate, then retrace the route (or observe the investigation a second time) with a disabled escort, discussing which things truly constitute barriers.

Investigations needn't limit your allies to the here and now, either — they can extend for days. One successful awareness event gave allies the task of pretending on the phone to be disabled and trying to hire a personal care assistant by calling a number of agencies. The session began on a Saturday with an introductory session. The allies were given their instructions and sent away to do their investigation during the week. The next Saturday they met with escorts again to discuss their findings.

There's no better way to get allies to learn about the ways in which disabled people are put at a disadvantage by our social institutions than by having them try to do the many many things disabled people are forced to do by rules, regulations, policies for "special" programs: It's an amazingly effective short course in how society "medicalizes" the lives of people who have disabilities but who are not "sick."

**Here are some kinds of investigations your allies can carry out:**

☛ Try to find out how to sign up for the local "paratransit" service.

☛ Try to get a personal care assistant from an agency.

☛ Try to learn about getting Social Security disability benefits.

☛ Try to find out how to get an official ID if you can't drive a car.

☛ Try to find out how you can cast your ballot if you can't see the voting machine.

☛ Try to find out if a public hearing will have an interpreter. You're deaf; you can't use the phone. Try to do it by email or website. If that doesn't work, go in person to the public agency and try to ask the question using pen and paper. Later, discuss what you'd do if you could neither read nor write.

☛ Try to find out if that public hearing you want to attend will have a sign-language interpreter, because your friend, who's deaf, wants to attend the hearing as well.

Both before and after such an investigation, escorts should talk about how disabled people are so often required to have a doctor's statement for "special" programs.

**Other useful discussions might ask these questions:**

☛ How did you feel as you tried to get this or that "benefit"? Were these feelings there when you started your investigation, or did they result from the interactions you had with the people you contacted? What is this about?

☛ Are "special" programs necessary? If so, why? Whom do they benefit? Whom do they restrict? How does power function in such transactions? Who has the power? Who's the "supplicant"?

☛ Could there be other ways to do things? Could "special" be avoided? How does prejudice come into play here?

☛ Does the system feel discriminatory? How could it be changed? What do you want to do about this insight? Is this something you want to take on as a social change objective with other allies and escorts? How does that decision make you feel?

☛ Is any of what you ran into actually illegal? (Escorts should know the answers to this before assigning the investigation). If it is illegal, what do you want to do about it? Is this something you want to take on as a social change objective with other allies and escorts? How does that decision make you feel?

## Dramatization and role-playing

Though similar, dramatization and role-playing, as this handbook uses the terms, are different activities: A dramatization is something allies watch. It's staged by others, who have rehearsed — typically a disabled escort and a non-disabled activist A role-play is something allies participate in, without any rehearsal.

A dramatization, followed by role-playing with allies, is a good way to teach awareness of prejudice and discrimination, particularly when the issue isn't something visual like the lack of a ramp or websites that contain information only in graphic form. A dyslexic person encounters prejudice in a classroom from a professor who doesn't believe the student's problem is real. A person with chemical sensitivities requests a hotel room that's scent-free; she's ignored by the manager, who becomes angry when she complains.

At an event using dramatization and role-playing, the dramatization comes first. Allies watch as a disabled escort faces discrimination at the hands of a bigoted bureaucrat. Disabled escorts create the script, making sure the bigot's and the disabled person's lines are both realistic and unambiguous.

Role-playing follows the dramatization. An ally takes the role of a disabled person, an escort plays the bureaucrat. Afterwards, the ally talks with the group of allies and escorts about how the experience felt. Following this, another ally plays the bureaucrat prejudiced against the disabled person, played by the escort. Again, the point of the activity is to allow the ally to discuss feelings. What did it feel like to be told they weren't allowed to do this or that? How did it feel when the reason the bureaucrat gave seemed unfair or illegal? Reversing things, how did it feel to be able to "enforce" a rule that affected a disabled person's life? Did you feel the disabled person was being unreasonable, wanting too much, being whiny? What caused those feelings? Could bigotry have a role in them? Did the bigotry seem reasonable because, after all, that's "how the system is set up"? Or "too bad, those are the rules"?

Depending on time constraints, everyone can take turns role-playing — or a few allies can volunteer to perform for the group.

It's important that the group watch a dramatization first, because this provides a model for the behavior. Creative and talented activists might film a dramatization and show the film to the group — but the key to this type of awareness event is that allies get to see a model of the bigoted behavior, and the response, prior to the role-play. That's why the dramatization comes first.

Creating dramatizations takes talent and work. If your escorts have had some experience in theater, or can get help from friends who have theater experience, dramatization followed by role-playing might be a good technique to try. Otherwise, stick to one of the other techniques.

Like everything else concerning Awareness Days, dramatization and role-playing will only achieve the intended result if they're preceded by a session explaining the point and followed by a period in which allies get to process what they've witnessed.

## Audiovisuals

There are a number of good films about the disability experience that could be used quite well as an awareness event all by themselves, without any other activity. We've listed some in Appendix C, along with websites that offer many more choices.

Be aware that if your escorts or your allies include people who are blind, audiovisual isn't the activity to use. Be sure to think about this first, before you decide on this activity. Hearing-impaired participants will need captioned films.

Readers of this manual surely know by now that a film's usefulness as a way to educate allies about ableism depends almost entirely on the preparation the audience has, and their processing of it afterwards.

Always, always, always plan for three parts to your awareness event:

1. An introduction beforehand, presenting the issues the audience will encounter in the film (suggestions of "things to watch for" are always useful)

2. The film itself

3. The discussion afterwards, led by disabled allies.

If you do plan to use a film (or films) for your awareness event, be sure your escorts prepare by watching the films beforehand and deciding on how to discuss them with the allies before and after the showing.

A word to the wise. A captioned film is always better than a non-captioned film; open-captioning is best. Do not assume that none of your allies or escorts need captioning!

## Fun activities

There's nothing wrong with fun activities.

For an awareness event at her university, says law student Bethany Stevens, "we hosted mini-drag races of able-bodied people using wheelchairs":

"At no point in the activity did anyone extol the idea that people could garner what it is really like to be disabled," says Stevens, "but it did elucidate a very important part of disability, one that is not often discussed: that disability is not all bad, and some aspects of being disabled can actually be fun!

"As a wheelchair user, I honestly get a lot of joy riding quickly down a hill with wind in my hair." This is something Stevens says she wanted to share with non-disabled students, because it's one of the ways to show that being in a wheelchair is not *in and of itself* a horrible thing.

## Try this exercise!

**Discuss how this wheelchair drag-racing activity differs from the ones Beth Ferri witnessed (page 21) in which organizers laughed at the mishaps of the blindfolded people having difficulty navigating a path.**

**Does the difference have something to do with being included in an activity organized by disabled people for their own enjoyment?**

**Does the difference have something to do with sharing, with equality, with power relationships?**

## Discussion sessions

Discussion should bracket any activities your participants engage in: Honest, open discussion, between equals: the participant allies and the disabled escorts.

"It is the collective and brutally honest processing" of the Awareness Day activity that brings the results, stresses Meghan L. Todd of Sarah Lawrence College. Todd, who calls herself a "women's historian and disability rights advocate," is one of those who believe simulations in and of themselves simply don't work. The activity, whatever it is, is only the fodder for the discussion, which is where the learning occurs.

Many disability rights experts say one should forget about the simulation aspect altogether and just discuss the idea of simulations! It's a clever idea.

Prof. Art Blaser shows you 10 ways you can do this.

"What are the kinds of experiences that only a non-disabled person simulating a disabled one would have?

"What are simulations designed to do? Is that a desirable objective?"

"Do they really accomplish that objective? Why, or why not?"

Read his entire article on page 109 for ideas for how to structure your own "simulation without simulation" event.

Prof. Ferri, who also doesn't think simulations are a good idea, uses topics for her discussion that are well-suited to her audience of students who are going to be teachers. The discussions below make sense in a college classroom, but the idea can be modified to suit almost any group and any situation.

"Early in the course I have my students [disabled and non-disabled alike] write about their earliest memories of disability. We then share these stories in small groups and make connections between our various stories.

"We talk about how many of their stories are 'home' or 'neighborhood' stories compared to 'school' stories. It has been interesting to see slightly more 'school' stories emerge in the years I have been doing this activity — a trend toward inclusion, no doubt.

"Often students talk about how neighborhood friends simply disappeared once they got to school or moved on to the middle grades. They wonder as adults why they didn't question this disappearance at the time."

Structured discussions like these often get your participants much further along in understanding than simulations do. The key for successful discussions — ones that lead to action — is for you and your disabled escorts to plan the discussions beforehand. What questions will be posed? What are some of the possible range of responses non-disabled people might make? What kinds of responses will the disabled escorts likely have to the same discussion questions? How do these differ, and what accounts for the difference? Posing this kind of a follow-up question is as useful, if not more useful, than the initial question that began the discussion. It's also useful to have handouts that supplement and enrich the discussion. Often it's better to save these to hand out at the end, for participants to take home and reflect on in light of what they've talked about during the session.

What *does* happen to the neighborhood friends with disabilities, anyway? The discussion Ferri's students have about this can be nicely supplemented, for example, by Harriet McBryde Johnson's New York Times Magazine article, "The Disability Gulag" (online at http://www.protectionandadvocacy-sc.org /Disability%20Gulag.htm when this book went to press.)

## Try this exercise!

**Using the articles in Appendix D, figure out the kinds of discussions your escorts and allies can have that each article could supplement. Then provide the article at session's end.**

Don't forget to provide discussion handouts in large print — easily done by using the sizing function on any copier or by downloading it from the website. And be sure to give participants the website URL as well, where they can access it themselves in a format that works best for them.  See Appendix B for specific information about providing a choice of formats for participants.

"Students often talk about relatives who had disabilities, but how they had not thought of them in terms of the category—they were just Uncle Bill," says Ferri. "We talk about the lack of disabled people in their lives given that people with disabilities constitute the largest minority group in this country."

Pages 28 and 99 in this handbook make some points about this issue, and it would certainly make a good discussion starter for an Awareness Day session. It's a topic that can take people in many useful directions, as this anecdote told by disability scholar suggests:

> I recall being told quite bluntly by a faculty member there were no people with disabilities in the department. "And certainly no faculty or staff with disabilities!" he huffed, as he limped off on a braced leg damaged by post-polio syndrome, in his hand a sheaf of paperwork denying assistance to a blind student who attended classes with her guide dog.

Many of the discussion ideas in this handbook come from disability studies professors, who in general believe discussion trumps simulation any day as a way to learn about disability. But professors, of course, are used to handling discussions and are often skilled at directing the flow of ideas. Good professors also watch for hurt feelings and escalating emotions. "These conversations are inevitably emotionally charged, unsettling, and painful — and also more complex" than simulation, says Todd. Good discussion facilitators know how to defuse tense situations and, just as important, how to move the discussion along so that participants feel comfortable being open and honest in their feelings and comfortable with the give-and-take that's essential if any real learning is to take place.

If neither you nor your disabled escorts know techniques for facilitating good discussion, it's really important to use a trained facilitator to serve that function for your Awareness Day. They may offer to volunteer, or you may need to pay for their services. But a skilled discussion facilitator is worth every penny you spend. On page 46 we look at what you'll need to do to prepare a discussion facilitator for the work she'll be doing on your Awareness Day.

Ferri offers other discussion topics that you might like to use as well:

> We talk about our own university classroom and what kind of bodies it was designed for. We talk about the institutional chairs (with desk attached) and how the desk was designed with the 'normal' body in mind. We find that none of our bodies seem to fit comfortably in these chairs — and this leads us to talk about what a fiction "normal" really is. We ponder what a universally designed classroom might look like — and, why is it that the classroom designers feel so comfortable designing spaces that are by their very structures exclusionary.

> We also work on curriculum — I try to get them to see that inclusive classrooms are not just about who is in the room, but also about what is being taught....

Use these discussion examples to create your own discussion scenarios.

# Chapter 9
# Beyond Awareness Day:
# Ongoing work and support

We learned in our look at "institutionalized prejudice" in Chapter 1 that when we truly want to change other's attitudes, it's crucial that our institution change its ableist policies and behavior.

Your organization may say it supports your awareness work. But will it "put its money where its mouth is?" Is it going to change its discriminatory policy, its discriminatory behavior? Is Podunk Community College actually going to install automatic doors?

Your escorts and allies want to continue their work beyond Awareness Day. They want change to occur. Fresno's activists wanted their city officials to do more than "experience" the broken curb cuts, heavy doors and hostile citizens angry at their presence in a public building (see article on page 111 ). They wanted those officials to change things in Fresno.

How will you ensure that your organization carries through? If the institution you want to change isn't your own organization but another target, will your organization provide support for your group to get the job done?

At the end of 3H-ABC's Awareness Day, escorts and allies were talking about a plan to get all of the community's officials to agree to a deadline for getting their sites accessible. The group wanted to form an informal ad-hoc committee and continue to meet. They'd need to send letters to city officials to begin the campaign. They'd need an accessible place for their meetings; they'd often need a sign-language interpreter. In this case, 3H was more than happy to offer organizational support for this work.

Your organization, if it's truly committed to the work to end ableism, should be willing to make a similar commitment to your Awareness Day participants.

## Time-tested activism tactics

Activist groups in most social change movements have developed tactics to "keep the pressure on" to ensure that change occurs — that their "demands are met," to use the language of social activism.

Most of these are simply common-sense:

**1. Define a "target"** ("the bad guy"). You really should name a person as a "target". "The Podunk Community College administration" is too vague a target. You need someone who's accountable, whose feet you can hold to the fire. Name a person. Who signs off ultimately on spending money for physical changes to the campus "plant"? That's the name you want. You want to personalize the "battle." You want a named target.

**2. Issue a demand or two** (the fewer the better). Demand a specific action, done by a specific date. Make sure it's concrete, an action whose completion can actually be verified. In other words, don't demand that the administration "promise to install doors" — after all, they can "promise" anything. A promise isn't what you're aiming for. You want the work done. Your demand should be for "automatic doors installed at the front entrance to Merritt Hall by Sept. 15 (March 15, July 31, etc.)."

**3. Keep the pressure on**. Target the target. Don't let up. Be noisy. Remind your audience of your demand. Keep tabs on progress. Issue public statements. Form a picket line if you have to. Hold a protest, make signs. Send mass emails. Create a website for campus supporters to sign a petition.

One of the best and easiest-to-follow primers on doing this kind of activist work is Saul Alinsky's *Rules for Radicals*. You and your escorts may want to read it as you prepare for Awareness Day.

And it makes a great gift for your new allies at the first meeting of your new project group.

# Chapter 10
# Your Countdown Calendar

## At least 9 months before your awareness event

1. Define a goal (pp 36).

2. Begin your education. (pp 41).

3. Meet with disability student groups or activist groups (pp 43).

4. Determine the venue: select the location for the event to be held.

> **Ensure that it is completely accessible. Remember, you are providing a model for the allies who will be participating.**

## "Accessible" means:

☛ full wheelchair access (including automatic doors or doors that can be propped open, or a "doorman" stationed at the entrance to the room and to restrooms during the event)

☛ sign language interpreters

☛ materials in various formats. Appendix B tells you how to do this.

☛ scent-free space

☛ access to natural light or incandescent lighting (fluorescent lighting adversely affects people with some kinds of neurological disabilities).

Other access accommodations can include real-time captioning provided on an A-V screen, personal readers and roving attendants/gofers who can assist people whose limited hand function makes it impossible to turn pages; assist people in the restroom and during lunch, etc. And see Appendix F for a checklist to determine that the meeting space is accessible.

## "Do we have to?"

"But if I know nobody in the group needs all this! Why should we spend time and money to provide it?" you ask.

The answer:

> **Your event serves as a model to those participating of what nondiscrimination should look like. If you're reluctant to create an accessible environment for your event, this might be a good time for you to ask yourself about your own commitment to equality.**

It might be time to take a look at the kinds of subtle ableist thinking we're all subject to. If your organization's decision-makers balk at providing an accessible space for the event ("It will cost too much! It takes too much time to do! Nobody needs all that access!") you might think about how to structure an awareness event to raise the consciousness of those decision-makers.

## 4 to 6 months prior to your event

1. Recruit disabled escorts.

2. Continue "self-education" with escorts. Read this manual, read the articles in the Appendices, and work to develop a shared consciousness about ableism.

3. Decide on your target audience and recruitment process.

4. Make a detailed plan for what will be needed to make your meeting space accessible.

5. Determine if any of your escorts have training in facilitating discussion sessions; if not, begin search for trained discussion facilitators.

## 2 to 4 months prior to your event

1. Meet with escorts to plan the objective of the event.

2. Plan

   ☛ the initial session

   ☛ the activity

   ☛ the discussion follow-up

3 Determine materials needed (if any); props, handouts, etc. If renting a film, order it to be sure you'll have it available.

4. Hire a discussion facilitator if one is needed (see page 46.).

5. Hire interpreter, personal readers, roving attendants.

6. If necessary (see next chapter), begin initial publicity efforts to recruit target audience.

7. Will you have food? Snacks? Make arrangements for any catering.

## 1 month prior to your event

1. Check on any props needed.

2. Prepare handouts for the event, remembering to produce them in formats accessible to all participants.

3. Begin pre-registration or registration. If participants sign up beforehand, be sure to ask them to list any accommodation needs. Even though you're targeting non-disabled people, don't be surprised if some turn out to actually have accommodation needs.  Sometimes having participants do some preliminary work beforehand can be helpful. You can provide brief materials to read when they register. A simple way to do this is to send them materials by email. This has the added advantage of being accessible to everyone who uses email. Some people may not have email, though, so you should also be prepared to mail

materials. Keep any advance materials very brief. You don't want to over-whelm your participants at the start.

4. Check on catering and other logistics. **Do any escorts need transportation to the event?** Accessible transportation is iffy at best. You don't want to learn the morning of Awareness Day that 5 of your 17 escorts have been stranded at their homes by a paratransit provider that failed to show up. It's best to have some sure transportation plan in place — maybe the escorts with lift-equipped vans can pick others up. Make sure some definite arrangements have been made so your escorts arrive on time!

## In the final days leading up to your Awareness Day...

1. Confirm the day's agenda and process with escorts, making sure everyone knows their role, discussions have been mapped out, etc.

2. Finalize logistics — catering, transportation for escorts. Have the rental videos arrived? Have you and your escorts previewed them and developed discussion questions?

3. Double-check your list of gofers and other workers; make sure you have enough people on hand to be assistants. (Better too many than not enough!)

4. Double-check the access of the event space (see Appendix E) and materials.

5. Relax — and get ready to have fun! Your Awareness Day is going to be a great success!

# Chapter 11
# Marketing and media

Who should know about your Awareness Day?

The 3H-ABC partnership decided early on that they didn't really need to do any outside publicity for their awareness event. Their own volunteers were the target audience, and they were already required to participate in one of the organization's training days each year. The volunteers received emails about the event, describing the organization's goal and a bit about the activity they'd be undertaking. But since it wasn't an event open to the public, they didn't send out news releases or seek media coverage. All they needed to do was to register the participants, which they did online.

If your awareness event is designed specifically for your own members, or if it's a "by invitation only" event, publicity needn't be a concern.

The architects whose training we read about earlier had responded to letters inviting them to participate in an Awareness Course. A group of public officials such as the ones who took part in Fresno's Awareness Day should also be invited individually. In neither of these cases do you really need to do "publicity" about your event.

Many Awareness Day organizers, however, hope their events can do double-duty and educate "the public," even when "the public" isn't being invited to participate in the event. They think a story in the media about the event will in itself educate the public. They hope that reporters will write about the day's activities in a way that gives the public some "awareness" too.

Because of this, many Awareness Day planners invite members of the media to be participants.

There are some real pitfalls to this approach, however. On page 16 we read some quotes from a reporter who participated in an awareness event. The resulting article, "A Lesson in Empathy," though written with the best of intentions, exhibits traces of the kind of "unintended learning" that activists worry so much about with disability simulations. The writer, Lance Crossley, focused quite a bit on those things participants were no longer able to do:

"At one of the first stations we are told to do up two buttons on a dress shirt," writes Crossley. "Seems simple enough, but the shirt is white, as are the buttons, and my cataracts don't allow me to discern the contrast [Crossley has been outfitted with goggles that simulate having cataracts]. Even when I do locate them, the lack of sensation in my hands makes it difficult to put the button through the slit. I do one button up and tell my partners that I did both. They can't see it anyway.... "

"Becoming sensitive and understanding this kind of suffering" was the purpose of the simulation event, Crossley wrote. But were *Halliburton Echo* readers left with more sensitivity and understanding, or simply left feel sad for older people who had so many problems with vision and fingers? Was this ultimately a good or a bad thing?

Joliet, IL Central High School journalism students, after participating in a "Disabled For A Day" event, got to write about the experience in Joliet's local newspaper. One wrote that "the worst part was knowing that many people have to endure this pain on a daily basis for the rest of their lives." Another says she had "briefly felt how it would feel to be wheelchair bound for life." Another "couldn't keep the tears from my eyes." Still another student told readers she was "grateful" for being able to remove her blindfold at the end of the event "because so many people do not have the option of taking off the blindfold." And readers were treated to this rendition of the common stereotype: "People with mental disabilities don't comprehend and learn like others, but they're care-free."

**Don't assume reporters (or journalism students) will miraculously escape learning from a simulation's hidden curriculum. And more than most people, these particular allies are quite skilled in putting their emotions into words for the public.**

Are these the beliefs and attitudes you want the public to adopt as a result of your Awareness Day?

Should you try to conduct your Awareness Day in secret, hidden away where reporters can't find you and report on your events? Of course not! Still, these examples show why simulations without context can be dangerous. They show why your event must have a "before" and "after"; why it must have disabled escorts who are prepared; and why it might be better to skip the "simulation" aspect altogether and stick with some of the other techniques, such as shadowing, investigation or dramatizations and role-playing which this manual outlines. And of course, as you have learned by now, you must bracket everything with well-planned discussions!

Although there are pitfalls to avoid with reporters, well-done media attention to disability issues is invaluable. After all, John Howard Griffin's *Black Like Me*, even though it irritates some African-Americans today, at the time greatly increased white people's awareness of racial discrimination. When members of the media become "aware" as a result of a well-done awareness event, their reporting shines a spotlight on ableism in a way few other efforts can match.

## Reporters as allies

Lilla Zuill, a reporter for the *Bermuda Sun*, seems to have decided on her own that the best way to learn about Bermuda's access problems was "to spend a few hours in a wheelchair."

Zuill wasn't getting into the wheelchair entirely unprepared, though. She had already talked with an official about the problems, and she had a clear objective: "to report first-hand on the accessibility issues facing people in wheelchairs."

She also had an escort: "Ann Lindroth, Government's newly-appointed Coordinator for Disabled Persons, agreed to spend some time 'exploring' Hamilton with me, to see just how easy — or not — it might be to get around the city by wheelchair."

More an investigation (p. 55) than a simulation activity, Zuill planned, once in her wheelchair, to take a taxi to meet Lindroth at her office, so she could see what it was like for wheelchair users who needed to take taxis.

And she found out:

> I was to meet Ms. Lindroth, at her office on Court Street, at 10 a.m., but so far had not been able to get a taxi.… I called Radio Cabs. A woman there, while very polite, explained that the dispatch usually takes advance orders for wheelchair taxis. She said that she would see what she could do for me, and I left her my contact number.
>
> Calling several other cab companies — ones advertised as wheelchair taxi services — did not prove any more fruitful. Although I called both the main numbers and cellular numbers of those providers, I was only able to get through to voice mail. I left messages, but did not get any calls back.
>
> After about 45 minutes, and not having heard from any of the wheelchair taxis or Radio Cabs  — whom I did an unsuccessful double check with — I was forced to temporarily abandon my wheelchair and drive into Hamilton in my own car.
>
> It made me wonder: How much longer would it have taken to get a wheelchair accessible cab — hours? Half-a-day? Longer?…

"Disabled people are penalized more by the inadequacy of facilities in Bermuda than by their physical limitations," she wrote. (When this book was being written, Zuill's article could still be found on the website of the *Bermuda Sun* at http://www.bermudasun.bm/main.asp?Search=1&ArticleID=6175&SectionID= 82&SubSectionID=231&S=21 )

Mary Burrell, a Florida newspaper editor, also decided to use a wheelchair — for a month! Like Zuill, Burrell was specifically investigating access: "two family members and I decided to take one month of personal experience with wheel-chairs and rate the local spots we frequented during that time."

Her initial idea, she wrote, was to find places with good access and feature them in the paper. Like many non-disabled people who sign up to attend Awareness Days, it doesn't occur to Burrell that things are as bad as they are. But like allies who participate in well-done awareness events, she quickly discovered that inaccessibility was rampant.

"Almost every facility we visited" had problems, she wrote.

"A fellow at the mall was riding his wheelchair in the middle of the lot last weekend because there was no lip in the curbing where he could get out of traf-fic. Handicapped [parking] spaces are often far away from the doors, the curbs are cut in an inconvenient spot down the walkway, or the lip in the curbing is at an odd angle to the door."

And she became angry about the discrimination: "Retail stores seem to put every obstacle possible in front of the disabled, from narrow aisles to doors that are difficult to open, to restrooms that are absolutely impossible to use when maneuvering in a wheelchair." (Burrell's article, "The spin on wheelchairs," was still on the Tampa Bay Newspapers, Inc. website when this book went to the printer — at http://www.tbnweekly.com/editorial/viewpoints/content_articles /010506_vpt-01.txt )

Did either woman's article change things in their communities? It would be interesting to find out.

As this book was going to press, a Ragged Edge reader alerted us to a column by *Tallahassee Democrat* Senior Writer Gerald Ensley. Headlined "No grumbling about the Americans with Disabilities Act," the article reported on what Ensley had discovered while disabled with a back injury. "One of the biggest lessons I learned was: Thank goodness for the ADA." The law was a "lifesaver" for him, he wrote. "It was a vivid lesson in how necessary those accommodations must be to people with disabilities — and a reminder that all of us are just an unexpected injury away from needing them ourselves."

None of these 3 newspaper staffers seems to have been involved in any kind of formal awareness event.

What does this mean? That learning can occur without awareness events? Absolutely.

Burrell's and Zuill's stories also offer us ideas for activities to suggest to reporters. Notice that each woman had a clear objective for becoming a temporary wheelchair user. Notice, too, that each stayed in a wheelchair for an extended period of time.

"To be in a wheelchair is still to be handicapped not so much by disability, but by the system," Zuill wrote after her experience.

Burrell saw this as well. "Every building with double doors — and without an automatic opener — should be retrofitted," she wrote. "How a person in a wheelchair is supposed to open one heavy door, I don't know. To have one door after another, like at fast food establishments, is just cruel." And Ensley called his experience "a vivid lesson in how necessary those accommodations must be."

These three people are becoming allies.

## Try this exercise!

**Go to http://www.news.google.com or some other news search engine like Yahoo. Using words like "wheelchair," try to locate some recent news stories by reporters who got into a wheelchair and investigated access.**

**How many news reporters are doing disability investigations and simulations? What are they learning? Are they reporting on "impairment" or "ableism"?**

**Try to find out if any reporters have done these kinds of investigations related to disabilities such as blindness or deafness. Discuss your findings.**

# Chapter 12
# Work for allies

When I first participated in anti-oppression/anti-racism training I was disturbed to discover just how deep my preconceived notions about ethnicity and gender ran.

Was such training painful? Absolutely.

Valuable? Without a doubt.

They don't call 'em "growing pains" for nothin'. The willingness to examine our prejudices is seldom, if ever, easy for anyone.

— *Lawrence Carter-Long, Disabilities Network of New York City*

"Several times recently my able-bodied partner of 7 years has mentioned to me how much he has changed, and how much his awareness of disability issues has changed, since being in a relationship with me," says Susan Fitzmaurice. "He notices articles in the newspapers relative to disability issues he never would have even glanced at before. He has demanded that in his work disability issues be addressed. He notes inaccessible features of buildings he goes to. He has expanded his definition of what it means to a person who is happy and fulfilled in their life."

Fitzmaurice's description of what has happened with her partner is a good description of what happens to people who are introduced to disability issues the right way, by disability activists. When we talk about creating allies through awareness events, what we're aiming for are non-disabled people who are not merely "more aware" or "more educated." We hope to actually change people, so that they, too, begin to engage in the work to end ableism and create an accessible society.

Fitzmaurice's partner was not isolated or insensitive before, she points out. "He was simply a man who had no personal experience with disability on a day-to-day basis."

And his changed consciousness "did not happen in one day, or even in one year," she continues. "It happened as a result of being in a relationship with me and truly walking/rolling the walk of disability with me over time.

"He is still putting pieces together."

Awareness Day activities, even simulations, are "essentially passive," Fitzmaurice says. "If you play gimp for a day and then go back to your life as it was and nothing changes, then nothing has been accomplished."

## A little history

Until recently it was simply assumed that non-disabled people knew what was best for "the disabled." The first systematic social efforts to "help the handicapped" came from charities and religious groups. In the 20th Century government began to assume that role, particularly after World War I as many injured soldiers returned to the U.S.

In the wake of the civil rights and other social movements of the 1960s, disabled people began asserting their right to speak for themselves and to insist on decision-making power over programs that affected their lives. The slogan "nothing about us without us" became a rallying cry. (A good book that offers an overview of this development is Joseph P. Shapiro's *No Pity*.)

And just as black power separatists of the later civil rights years took issue with the integrationist approaches of leaders like Rev. Martin Luther King, Jr., who welcomed whites and encouraged them to march alongside blacks, many disability rights activists of the 1970 and 1980s disliked and sometimes were hostile to non-disabled people involved directly in disability rights work.

Disabled activists argued, with justification, that non-disabled people too often assumed that it was they should be in charge; that they knew better than disabled people what was needed. Disability activists accused non-disabled people of paternalism.

And many of the accusations were true. They were certainly true when it came to the many social service program "for the handicapped" run by well-meaning but essentially clueless non-disabled "do gooders." (Read Billy Golfus on Do Gooders at http://www.mouthmag.com/do_goodertrouble.htm and http://www.tell-us-your-story.com/do1.html ) Mouth magazine (http://www.mouthmag.com) is a virtual repository of cautionary tales about do-gooders and the havoc they wreak in the lives of disabled people.

And so now we come to the end of our Awareness Day. We have raised the consciousness of non-disabled participants. Are they still do-gooders or have we convinced them to become allies?

What's the difference?

Allies and do-gooders are opposites, says one activist. "Do-gooders tell disabled people what to do. Allies take their direction from us. Do-gooders think they know how to run our lives. Allies know we're the authorities on our own lives, our own movement, our own fight for access and equality."

Another activist says being an ally is "all about the power relationship. With allies, you're equals, working together for a common goal."

To become allies, all of us must recognize that disabled activists are the authorities on their lives. They're the ones experiencing the discrimination. Their stories and insights must be respected. This is the ground rule. Adhering to this rule, allies work together toward a common goal of justice.

The following strategies for winning allies and working with them are adapted from materials by Ricky Sherover-Marcuse, who led "unlearning racism" workshops in the 1970s and 1980s. Trained in sociology and philosophy, Sherover-Marcuse was the wife of the German philosopher Herbert Marcuse; her workshops were an outgrowth of the reevaluation co-counseling movement.

**Both of the lists below might make useful handouts for your escorts and allies after your Awareness Day.**

## Ten reminders for escorts seeking allies

1. Assume that your group and that you in particular deserve allies.

2. Assume that your issues are justifiably of concern to all people outside of your group.

3. Assume that people in other groups are your natural allies, assume that all people outside your group want to be allies for you and that it is in their interest for them to do so.

4. Assume that it is only other people's own oppression and internalized oppression that prevents them — temporarily — from being effective allies to you at all times.

5. Assume that your allies are doing the best they can at the present time,  given their own oppression and internalized oppression. Assume that they can and will do better.

6. **Assume that you are the expert on your own experience and that you have information which other people need to hear.**

7. Speak from your own experience — without comparing your oppression to theirs.

8. Assume that your experience is also an experience of victories; be sure to share these— as well as the stories of how things are hard.

9. Expect perfection from your allies; expect them to be able to deal with "difficult issues" in your struggle. Assume that allies make mistakes; be prepared to be disappointed, and continue to expect the best from them.

10. Assume that you have a perfect right to assist your allies to become more effective for you. Assume that you can choose to do this at any time. Take full pride in your ability to do this.

## Twelve rules for being an effective ally

1. Assume that all people in your own group, just like you, want to be allied with disabled people facing prejudice and discrimination. Assume that you in particular are good enough and smart enough to be an effective ally. (This does not mean that you have nothing more to learn — see no. 6 below.)

2. **Assume that you have a perfect right to be concerned with disabled people's access and justice issues, and that it is in your own interest to do so. You may yourself be disabled some day, so it makes sense to join with disabled people as an ally.**

3. Assume that all people in the disability group want members of your group —

and you in particular — as an ally. Assume that they recognize you as such — at least potentially.

4. If you feel you are being rejected as an ally, recognize that this is the result of disabled people's experience of oppression and internalized oppression.

5. Assume that people in the disability group are already communicating to you in the best way they can at the present time. Assume that they can and will do better. Think about how to assist them in this without making your support dependent upon their "improving" in any way. (Hint: think about what has been helpful for you when you were in their position.)

6. Assume that disabled people are experts on their own experiences, and that you have much to learn from them. Use your own intelligence and your own experience to think about what disabled people might find useful.

7. Recognize that as a non-disabled person you are an expert on the experience of having been conditioned to take the ableist role. This means that you know the content of the lies which disabled people have internalized. Don't let timidity force you into pretended ignorance.

8. Recognize that disabled people are survivors and that they have a long history of resistance. Become an expert on this history (see pages 76 and 84) and assist disabled people to take full pride in it.

9. Work to learn as much as you can about issues of concern to disabled people, especially the issues which are most closely tied to their internalized oppression. Assume that your making mistakes is part of the learning process of being an ever more effective ally. Be prepared for flare-ups of disappointment and criticism. Acknowledge and apologize for mistakes, learn from them, but don't retreat.

10. Recognize that disabled people can spot "ableist conditioning;" do not bother with trying to "convince" them that this conditioning did not happen to you. Don't attempt to convince disabled people that you are "on their side;" just be there.

11. Do not expect gratitude" from disabled people; thoughtfully interrupt if it is offered to you. Remember, being an ally is a matter of your choice. It is not an obligation; it is something you get to do.

12. Be a 100 percent ally; no deals; no strings attached: "I'll oppose ableism." Period.

# Part 3:
# Resources and readings

# Appendix A: Ready resources

## General disability community websites

**Ragged Edge Online**: news, blogs, commentary and a big, big searchable archive of articles from the folks behind this handbook
http://www.raggededgemagazine.com

**Ouch!** UK's premiere crip website, powered by the BBC: http://www.bbc.co.uk/ouch/

**Mouth** magazine: irreverent, hard-hitting "voice of the disability nation":
http://www.mouthmag.com

**Disability Studies, Temple U. blog:** Always interesting and new stuff about disability rights and culture   http://disstud.blogspot.com/

## Quick stats: Americans with disabilities

**From the U.S. Census Bureau's press office (May, 2006):**

About 18 percent of Americans ( 51.2 million) say they have a disability. Nearly 12 percent (32.5 million) say they have a severe disability.

About 56 percent of people ages 21 to 64 who had a disability were employed at some point in the one-year period prior to the interview. People with a severe disability status reported the lowest employment rate (42 percent). This compared with the employment rates of people with a non-severe disability (82 percent) and those with no reported disability (88 percent).

Similarly, 32 percent of people ages 25 to 64 with a non-severe disability and 22 percent with a severe disability were college graduates. The corresponding rate for those without a disability was 43 percent.

☛ Four million children ages 6 to 14, or 11 percent, had a disability. The chances of having a disability rise with age: 72 percent of people age 80 and older had disabilities.

☛ Approximately 11 million people ages 6 and older, or 4 percent, needed personal assistance with an everyday activity. Among the population age 15 and older, 2.7 million used a wheelchair and 9.1 million an ambulatory aid such as a cane, crutches or a walker.

☛ About 7.9 million people age 15 and older had difficulty seeing the words and letters in ordinary newspaper print, including 1.8 million who were unable to see.

☛ There were 7.8 million people age 15 and older who had difficulty hearing a normal conversation, including 1 million unable to hear.

☛ About 14.3 million people age 15 and older had limitations in cognitive functioning or a mental or emotional illness that interfered with their daily activities, such as Alzheimer's disease, depression or mental retardation. This was 6 percent of the population.

☛ Among adults ages 16 to 64, 11.8 million or 6 percent reported the presence of a condition that makes it difficult to remain employed or find a job.

☛ Median earnings for people with no disability were $25,000, compared with $22,000 for people with a non-severe disability and $12,800 for those with a severe disability.

☛ Of those ages 15 to 64, 36 percent with a severe disability used a computer and 29 percent used the Internet at home.

The Census defines a person as "having a disability" if they have difficulty performing a specific activity such as seeing, hearing, bathing or doing light housework, or have a specified condition, such as Alzheimer's disease or autism. People are considered to have a severe disability if they are completely unable to perform one or more of these tasks or activities, need personal assistance or have one of the severe conditions described in Census reports.

These data were collected from June through September 2002 in the Survey of Income and Program Participation. As in all surveys, these data are subject to sampling variability and other sources of error. This information is online at  http://www.census.gov /Press-Release/www/releases/archives/aging_population/006809.html

## Fun disability history websites

**The Smithsonian National Museum of American History**'s Disability Rights Movement online interactive exhibit gives a good overview for people not familiar at all with recent disability rights history, and it's a fun web activity.
http://americanhistory.si.edu/disabilityrights/welcome.html

**The Disability Social History Project** is run by two Californians long active in disability rights.  http://www.disabilityhistory.org/

Disability history timeline http://www.disabilityhistory.org/timeline_new.html

**The Disability History Museum** at http://www.disabilitymuseum.org offers an extensive document library at http://www.disabilitymuseum.org/lib/docs/

## University programs in disability studies

**"Disability Studies" is a term with wide-ranging interpretations. Not all university-level disability studies programs are equal in quality or focus. Many are still housed within traditional "medical-model" departments and programs.**

 **Below is a brief selection of programs around the country. This is by no means a complete list. Visit http://disabilitystudies.syr.edu/resources/programsinds.aspx for a more extensive (and, hopefully, updated) list.**

The City University of New York offers a Graduate Certificate in Disability Studies from their School of Professional Studies.
http://sps.gc.cuny.edu/programs/certificate.html#multidisciplinary

Gallaudet University in Washington, DC offers a Master's of Arts in Deaf Studies.
http://depts.gallaudet.edu/Deaf.Studies/

Ohio State University offers an undergraduate minor in disability studies and a graduate interdisciplinary specialization in disability studies. http://disabilitystudies.osu.edu/

Ryerson University in Toronto offers a Bachelor's of Arts in Disability Studies from its School of Disability Studies. Also has some distance education courses in disability studies. http://www.ryerson.ca/ds/

Syracuse University in Syracuse, NY offers both a Master's and Ph.D. concentration in Disability Studies through its School of Education.
http://disabilitystudies.syr.edu

Teachers College, Columbia University in New York City offers a Master of Arts in Disability Studies in Education (DSE).
http://www.tc.edu/C&T/Disability-Studies/detail.asp?id=Program+Description

Temple University in Philadelphia offers a Graduate Certificate in Disability Studies through its Institute on Disabilities.
http://disabilities.temple.edu/programs/ds/

Washington State University in Pullman, WA, offers an Undergraduate Minor in Disability Studies through its Department of Speech and Hearing Sciences.
http://www.libarts.wsu.edu/speechhearing/academics/minor-ds.html

The University of California at Berkeley offers a Minor in Disability Studies.
http://ls.berkeley.edu/ugis/ds/

The University of Hawai'i at Manoa offers an Interdisciplinary Disability and Diversity Studies Certificate from its Center on Disability Studies.
http://www.cds.hawaii.edu/features/certificates.aspx

The University of Illinois at Chicago offers Master's and Ph.D. programs in disability studies from the College of Applied Health Sciences.
http://www.ahs.uic.edu/dhd/

The University of Toledo offers an Undergraduate Interdisciplinary Minor in Disability Studies and a Master's-level concentration in Disability Studies.
http://www.dstprg.utoledo.edu/

The University of Washington in Seattle offers a Disability Studies Minor through its Department of Political Science.
http://depts.washington.edu/disstud/index.html

## Finding an independent living center

Two useful listings of (in theory) all independent living centers across the U.S.:

**ILRU Directory** http://www.ilru.org/html/publications/directory/index.html

**The Independent Living USA** site has a useful directory and overview:
http://www.ilusa.com/links/ilcenters.htm

## Language guidelines

*A longer version of the guidelines below was developed in 1992 by The Advocado Press, Inc. under the title* **Beyond the AP Stylebook: Language and Usage Guide for Reporters and Editors***. They are available online at http://www.mediacircus.org/styleguide.htm*

**Two simple rules should be kept in mind when writing stories about people who have disabilities:**

**1. Avoid clichés and clichéd constructions.**

**2. Use "value-neutral" terms and constructions. Don't interject your admiration — or pity — into your story.**

### A GROUP — AND ITS TERMINOLOGY — IN EVOLUTION

People with disabilities do not agree on the best terms to use in describing themselves. In this they are similar to other minorities who did not settle on what they were to be called until their movement gained some prominence in the press. People who we once called "colored" or "Negro" we next called "black" and are now often referring to as "African-American." Until recently, the term of choice was "black." "Black" itself became accepted terminology only during the "black power" days of the Civil Rights movement. Prior to that, the "correct" term had been "Negro." "Colored" was also used. Years ago, of course, "nigger" was also used.

Today the word "nigger" is taboo. Yet, we know that some African-Americans will use the term "nigger" among themselves. We know, however, that the press is not to use it. And we adhere to that rule. We also know that some African-Americans, particularly elderly African-Americans, refer to themselves as "colored" or "negro." Yet we do not then use either of these terms in writing about them. The term still used by the news media often is "black" — although "African-American" is replacing it.

The disability community is still in the process of deciding how to refer to its members. Many new terms get tried out. Some people refer to themselves as "physically challenged" or "handicapable" or "inconvenienced"; others continue to refer to themselves as "victims" or "crippled." However, none of these terms is accepted by most disability rights activists.

### "DISABLED" AND "DISABILITY" TERMS OF CHOICE

Most people involved in disability issues today see "disabled" or "disability" as terms of choice. Many want journalists to write "person with a disability" rather than "disabled person." Disability studies scholars prefer "disabled person," i.e., someone disabled by society's discrimination. The terms "handicap" and "handicapped" have been used in legislation and during the 1960s and early 1970s, it was the word of choice. It fell into disrepute, however, when leaders of the disability rights movement insisted it was a term coined by professionals and not a term the movement chose. (It *does not* come from "cap in hand" signifying begging. See http://www.uhh.hawaii.edu/~ronald/HandicapDefinition.htm ). Today, most disability groups are changing the "handicap" in their titles to "disability."

### INSIDE TERMS:

Within the disability rights movement, individuals may refer to themselves as "crips," "gimps," "deafies," "paras," and "quads." These are "in" terms within the movement. While an interview subject may use them, they are still considered slang and are not ordinarily to be used by the press.

## GROUP TERMS:

While many prefer that journalists use "people (or persons) with disabilities," they accept "disabled people" as a substitute. The phrase "the disabled" is not good usage. Since "disabled" is an adjective, it's important to avoid ridiculous — and improper — constructions such as "disabled group" or "disabled rights" or "disabled transportation." Instead, build phrases using the word "disability." "the disability movement."

- ☛ "the disability rights movement"
- ☛ "disability activists"
- ☛ "disability advocates"
- ☛ "disability community"

When you're writing a housing story, you refer to the people affected as "residents." When writing an election wrap-up, you use the term "voters." Use these kinds of group nouns when referring to disabled people, too, to vary the "people with disabilities" phrase.

Possible terms could include:

- ☛ voters with disabilities
- ☛ disabled shoppers
- ☛ disabled travelers
- ☛ residents who have disabilities
- ☛ disabled opponents (or proponents)

Avoid terms beginning with "the" followed by an adjective, such as:

- ☛ "the disabled"
- ☛ "the blind"
- ☛ "the handicapped"
- ☛ "the retarded"

Instead, use:

- ☛ blind protesters
- ☛ deaf students
- ☛ people with head injuries
- ☛ people with disabilities

Avoid making nouns out of conditions. Don't write that someone was "a retard" or "a handicap" — even if your interview subject uses the term in this fashion.

## INAPPROPRIATE ADJECTIVES AND RIDICULOUS CONSTRUCTIONS

Frequently, one will see a term such as "handicapped parking" or "handicapped seating." The construction is incorrect. ("Disabled organization" is wrong, too.) Think through the concept to figure out a cleaner, more accurate way to express it. Some options include:

- ☛ accessible seating

☛ parking for disabled people

☛ disability organization

## Disability is not a fate worse than death.
## DON'T WRITE AS THOUGH IT WERE.

The single greatest harm done disabled people in writing about them is to give them the added emotional baggage of sensationalized words and phrases describing their disabling condition. It's done so much — and so unconsciously — that it creeps into the ordinary language used to refer to disability conditions. Some editors will insist, for example, that disabled people are "afflicted with" AIDS or are "victims" of multiple sclerosis. Gradually, however, more individuals with disabilities are insisting the language used to describe them be emotionally neutral.

Emotionally loaded language is to be avoided. Avoid using "suffers from," "afflicted with," "bound," "confined," "sentenced to," "prisoner," "victim," or any other term or colorful phrase that conjures up tragedy.

The goal is to write about people with disabilities in a nonjudgmental fashion. Simple terms like "had polio" should replace "suffers from" or "afflicted with." "In" or "uses a wheelchair" does nicely as a replacement for "prisoner of" or "confined to." Most of the time, no term at all is needed other than, perhaps a reference, if relevant to the story, that the person "uses a wheelchair" or "is deaf."

## SENTIMENTAL OR CUTE TERMS

Many trendy terms crop up that should be avoided. "Physically challenged," "inconvenienced," "differently abled" and "handi-capable" are among the more recent terms. They act as euphemisms and are best avoided. Stick to "disability" or" disabled." This also is true of terms such as "temporarily able-bodied." Stick to "non-disabled."

Many reporters and editors believe that if people have a disability, they must be heroic, courageous, inspiring, or special. These terms have become knee-jerk descriptors. Most disabled people resent having such language applied to them. Avoid referring to a person with a disability as "courageous," "heroic," "inspiring," "special," or "brave."

## "Overcoming" "in spite of"

Many journalists — and copy editors — feel no story about a disabled person should be without the terms "overcame her disability" or "in spite of his handicap." Beyond being trite and overworked, these terms inaccurately reflect the problems disabled people face.

Disabled people do not succeed "in spite of" their disabilities as much as they succeed "in spite of" an inaccessible and discriminatory society. They do not "overcome" their handicaps so much as "overcome" prejudice.

Using the term "overcome" inaccurately suggests that the task at hand is for a disabled person to somehow solve discrimination by himself or herself. This is much the same as suggesting a woman act like a man or a black person overcome race and try to act more white. The concepts themselves are flawed; they should be avoided.

## A "special" note

The term "special" as in "special education" has been, is, and will likely continue to be used to refer to programs provided to comply with federal law. However, the term "special" has come to be used as a euphemism for segregated programs or physical facilities that are almost always inferior to what is available to non-disabled individuals. "Special" has definite negative connotations within the disability rights movement.

If you are using the term "special" to mean "separate," use "separate" instead. Instead of writing, "special buses for the disabled," write, "separate buses for disabled people." For "special handicap bathroom," write, "separate bathroom."

If you are using the term "special" to mean "disabled," use "disabled" or "disability" instead.

In general, avoid the term, except when you must refer to it as part of a title, such as Special Olympics or Department of Special Education.

## IS YOUR PERSPECTIVE SHOWING?

If you get tired of using "person with a disability" and find it hard to come up with new ways to say "disabled person," ask yourself: Is any description needed at all?

Sometimes journalists unnecessarily refer to disability when it is not relevant to the story. Apply the same rules you'd use covering an African-American: If there's no impelling need to discuss the disability of the person in the story, leave it out.

## DON'TS AND DOS

- ☞ Don't use "victim of," "victim," "afflicted with," "suffers from," "stricken with." Do write, "has" if relevant to story; otherwise, don't use at all.

- ☞ Don't use "confined to a wheelchair." Do write, "in a (uses a) wheelchair."

- ☞ Don't use "wheelchair-bound," "prisoner of," "abnormal," "defective," "invalid." Use nothing; no term is needed.

- ☞ Don't use "special" bus, "special" bathroom. Do write, "separate bus," "segregated bathroom."

- ☞ Don't use "physically (or mentally) challenged." Do write, "person with a disability" or "disabled person."

- ☞ Don't use "inconvenienced." Do write, "person with a disability" or "disabled person."

- ☞ Don't use "handi-capable." Do write, "person with a disability" or "disabled person."

- ☞ Don't use "deaf-mute." Do write, "deaf"; "hearing impaired."

- ☞ Don't use "in spite of disability." Avoid the concept altogether.

- ☞ Don't use "overcame her handicap." Avoid the concept altogether.

- ☞ Don't use "handicapped parking." Do write, "accessible parking."

- ☞ Don't use "disabled seating." Do write, "seating for viewers in wheelchairs."

# Appendix B: How to provide 'alternative' formats for your handouts

**Any printed material you provide should also be provided as a routine matter in large print and electronically. You might consider using large print as your only format for printed materials, especially if handouts are not too long. Some people may request audio formats as well, and you may have some cassettes or iPods available at the registration desk as well.**

**As an option, you might consider providing materials only in electronic format, via a website (see below).**

## Large print

Large print documents are most readable if the body text is in 18-point type and headings are in 24-point type. Readability experts suggest a widely-used serif font like Times Roman for the body and a sans serif font like Arial for the headings.

You can produce materials in large print two ways:

☛ Enlarging a printed page using a photocopier or

☛ printing out a word-processing file on your computer printer in a larger font.

If you enlarge a page on a photocopier, be sure the paper in the copier is large enough so that all of the text gets on the page and isn't cut off at the edge.

In either case, use white paper with black printing for the best readability.

## Electronic formats

Providing handouts in electronic format gives participants the most flexibility in accessing the content in a format that's accessible to them. This is the ideal method for providing Awareness Day materials.

You can scan text from copyrighted material (book pages or magazine articles) using an OCR software program such as OmniPage — just make sure the copyright information is provided within the text file. This is no different than photocopying pages from a book to hand out at a workshop. Once you have turned printed text into an electronic text file, it can be "output" by the participant in many ways: by using a screen reader, converting it to large print, printing it out in Braille using a personal refreshable Braille display unit.

Warning: you cannot scan images of pages and provide them without first using OCR software. Scanned pages are graphic files and cannot be read by text-output software.

### *Things to remember when providing electronic files:*

Plain text (also called ascii, with an extension of .txt) is best. Files with .html or .rss or .xml extensions are also "device-independent" — which means they convert without special problems for a variety of output devices.

Try to avoid giving participants Word files (extension .doc) — not everyone uses the same version of Word, and this popular word-processing program inserts many "garbage" characters for its formatting. Word provides a "save as plain text" option which you should use to convert any .doc files to .txt files.

**Warning: Do not use PDF files. PDF files are graphics files and cannot be read by screen readers or converted for use with non-visual output devices.**

### Delivering electronic handouts to participants

If you have access to a website, upload the .txt or .html files onto the website, each with a separate file name. Create (or have your tech person create) an "index page" that links to each article.

If you don't have access to a website that you can post material on, consider creating an instant blog on one of the free blog sites such as blogger.com (name it something like <PodunkAwarenessHandouts> — blogger.com will create an automatic URL for your new site). Following the blogger.com instructions, enter each handout as an "entry" in the blog. Provide the blog's URL to participants and they can click on each entry to read the contents.

You may also want to burn a few CDs of the material to hand out at registration  for people who request them.

### Audio formats

Handouts can be read onto a standard cassette; the cassettes can be duplicated. This might be a good format to use for providing handouts to participants in advance; however  it is less useful for participants during discussions. Many people who cannot see print or who have not learned to read prefer audio formats. You might also make mp3 sound files for play on iPods.

It is important if you are making sound recordings for handouts to remember that  you must verbally describe any graphical information and must read out any material that appears in tables. If something must be omitted, the reader must note the omission verbally so the listener knows something is missing.

**At the time this book was written, the following two websites offered additional useful information about providing accessible formats:**

**http://www.disabilityresource.uic.edu/AlternativeFormat/ToolboxAltForm.txt**

**http://www.euroblind.org/fichiersGB/policy.htm**

# Appendix C: Books and movies

## Books

### General and anthologies

**The Disability Studies Reader,** edited by Lennard J. Davis (1997).

**The Ragged Edge: The Disability Experience from the Pages of the First Fifteen Years of The Disability Rag,** edited by Barrett Shaw (1994).

**Staring Back: The Disability Experience from the Inside Out,** Kenny Fries (ed.) (1997).

**Why I Burned My Book and Other Essays on Disability,** by Paul K. Longmore (2003).

### Memoirs

**Home Bound,** by Cass Irvin (2004).

**Moving Violations : War Zones, Wheelchairs, and Declarations of Independence**, by John Hockenberry (1995).

**My Body Politic,** by Simi Linton (2006).

**Too Late To Die Young,** by Harriet McBryde Johnson (2005).

### History and Current Affairs

**By Trust Betrayed: Patients, Physicians, and the License to Kill in the Third Reich**, by Hugh Gregory Gallagher (1990). This extensively researched study of the systematic murder of physically and mentally disabled people in the Third Reich raises troubling questions about many contemporary theories and ideas dealing with euthanasia, health care, and medical ethics.

**Christmas in Purgatory:** A photographic essay on mental retardation. by Burton Blatt and S. Kaplan A photographic exposé; of conditions in America's institutions. Shot with a hidden camera. Blatt was one of the few professionals to speak out against institutional warehousing in the 1960s.

**The Disability Rights Movement: From Charity to Confrontation**, by Doris Zames Fleischer and Frieda Zames (2001). Interviews with nearly 100 activists give a detailed history of the struggle for disability rights in the U. S.

**Deaf President Now!: The 1988 Revolution at Gallaudet University,** by John B. Christiansen and Sharon N. Barnartt (1995). "The actions of Gallaudet students later inspired me to challenge patronizing assumptions being made about my own community," writes disability activist Robin Orloff on the amazon.com website.

**FDR's Splendid Deception**, by Hugh Gregory Gallagher (1985, rev. 1994). Gallagher's account of the effort to conceal Roosevelt's disability from the public was the first book to take up this topic, igniting the fight to show FDR in his wheelchair.

**Forbidden Signs: American culture and the campaign against sign language,** by Douglas Baynton (1996) — "a rich history of the varied and sundry attempts that have been made to oppress the use of sign language."

**Mad in America: Bad Science, Bad Medicine, and the Enduring Mistreatment of the Mentally Ill,** by Robert Whitaker (2001). A medical journalist's disturbing look at the cruel and corrupt business of treating mental illness in America.

**Make Them Go Away: Clint Eastwood, Christopher Reeve and the case against disability rights,** by Mary Johnson (2003).

**The New Disability History: American Perspectives,** edited by Paul K. Longmore and Laurie Umansky (2001).

**No Pity: People with Disabilities Forging a New Civil Rights Movement,** by Joseph P. Shapiro (1994).

**To Ride the Public's Buses: The Fight that Built A Movement** (A Disability Rag Reader), edited by Mary Johnson and Barrett Shaw (2001).

### Sociology, Law, Political Science

**Americans with Disabilities: Exploring Implications of the Law for Individuals and Institutions,** edited by Leslie Pickering Francis and Anita Silvers (2000).

**The Making of Blind Men: A study of adult socialization,** by Robert A. Scott (1969). How agencies "for the blind" socialize people to think and act "blind."

**The Myth of Mental Illness,** by Thomas Szasz (1961).

**The Manufacture of Madness,** by Thomas Szasz (1970).

**Voices from the Edge: Narratives about the Americans with Disabilities Act,** edited by Ruth O'Brien (2004).

### Online book lists

**The Disability Studies: Information and Resources website from Syracuse University's Center on Human Policy offers a list of over 100 books and articles, with brief descriptions. A good source for those who wish to expand their education in disability movement theory. http://thechp.syr.edu/Disability_Studies_2003_current.html#books**

## Books referred to in this handbook

**All Rise: Somebodies, Nobodies and the Politics of Dignity,** by Robert Fuller (2006).

**Black Like Me,** by John Howard Griffin (1961)

**The Nature of Prejudice,** by Gordon Allport (1954).

**No Pity : People with Disabilities Forging a New Civil Rights Movement,** by Joseph P. Shapiro (1994).

**Rules for Radicals,** by Saul Alinsky (1971).

**Self-Made Man: One Woman's Journey into Manhood and Back,** by Norah Vincent (2006).

**Stigma: Notes on the Management of Spoiled Identity,** by Erving Goffman (1963).

## Movies, CDs, DVDs

There's no one "best" disability film. There are thousands of films with disabled characters. (Ironically, few of the disabled characters are played by actual disabled people, which might make an interesting Awareness Day discussion in itself.)

Below is a very short alphabetical selection of films, cds and dvds reviewed at Ragged Edge Online or recommended by readers.

**Before showing any film to Awareness Day participants, the cardinal rule is this: Screen it with your escorts to determine what discussion topics and points you want your allies to take from the film. Then plan your discussion. Always, always screen the film well before the Awareness Day, and work out the points that your escorts will be making in the post-film discussion. Where we've provided a link to a review, we strongly suggest reading the review first for ideas for discussion topics.**

**Autism Is A World** (2005), narrated by Sue Rubin, is "a direct attack on some of the most damaging ideas about autism, and it's a powerful statement about the value of communication," said our reviewer Cal Montgomery. "But where Rubin appears to believe that the problem is that autism limits her ability to function in the world, I believe that the problem is that the world is set up for neurotypical non-disabled people." Read our review at http://www.raggededgemagazine.com/reviews/ckmontrubin0605.html — DVD available from amazon.com

**The Color of Paradise** (1999) is "rich and arresting on many different levels," wrote our reviewer Anne Finger. "The sighted audience experiences a version of blindness, albeit temporarily. . . . . we see blind people being blind, not 'normalized' but fully and richly themselves, perceiving and interacting with the world in their own way." Read our review at http://www.raggededgemagazine.com/extra/colorofparadise.htm — film information at http://www.sonypictures.com/classics/colorofparadise/

**Going to School-Ir a la Escuela** (2001) "shares the daily experiences of students with disabilities who attend middle and elementary schools in Los Angeles, revealing the determination of parents to see that their children receive a quality education," says the Syracuse University disability studies site listed below. Movie info at http://richardcohenfilms.com/GoingtoSchool.htm

**How Difficult Can This Be? F.A.T. City —A Learning Disabilities Workshop** (1989). This Richard Lavoie documentary "shows a group of teachers/parents/aides being reduced to powerless, confused jelly in an excellent simulation of a learning environment that's hostile to people with learning disabilities," says Ragged Edge contributor Jesse Kaysen, who adds that it makes crystal-clear how "disability is a category created mostly by society." http://teacher.shop.pbs.org/product/index.jsp?productId=1863454&cp=2076319&view=all&parentPage=family

**If I Can't Do It** (1998). Arthur Campbell spent his first 38 years sheltered by overprotective parents at home. "I watched a lot of television," he says, "and I never saw a program about anyone whose life was like mine." Director Walter Brock follows Campbell into the heady activist environment of disability-rights rabble-rousers ADAPT, recording his fight for lifts on buses and his subsequent disillusionment. http://www.fanlight.com/catalog/films/258_iicdi.php

**Kiss My Wheels** (2003), an hour-long film about a kids' wheelchair basketball team from New Mexico, the Zia Hotshots, is "a film about kids learning that being different is OK, leaking catheters and falling out of wheelchairs are normal, and people who pick on wheelchair-using kids are nothing but bigots," wrote Josie Byzek in Ragged Edge Magazine. Film info at http://www.fanlight.com/catalog/films/367_kmw.php

**Murderball** (2005): "It's gritty, it's fast and it's a fascinating look at the quad jock lifestyle," wrote Susan LoTempio on the Ragged Edge Online website at http://www.ragged-edgemagazine.com/departments/reflections/000643.html   (Might be fun to watch along with Kiss My Wheels.)

**Titicut Follies** (1967), the classic film from director Frederick Wiseman, "reflects the barren existence of life in a mental hospital. . . . there is little regard for the inmates' human dignity," says the Syracuse University disability films listing; the film depicts strip searches, lack of privacy, ridicule, and isolation. http://www.subcin.com/titicut.html

**Twitch and Shout** (1995), directed by photojournalist Lowell Handler, who has Tourette's syndrome, takes a look at four people with Tourette's in a film that should make viewers "rethink notions of human value and individual differences," says the Syracuse University disability film site. http://www.blinddogfilms.com/twitchandshout/

**When Billy Broke his Head... And Other Tales of Wonder** (1995). TV journalist Billy Golfus, who sustained a traumatic brain injury, intercuts this first-person account with larger disability rights issues. http://fanlight.com/catalog/films/136_wbbhh.php

**X-Men: The Last Stand** (2006) was not particularly well-received by critics in the mainstream media. "And yet, from a disability perspective, it's one of the more complicated films to emerge from Hollywood in a long time," wrote George Washington University Prof. Robert McRuer on the Ragged Edge Online website. Read his review at http://www.raggededgemagazine.com/departments/frontpgfeature/001144.html

## Online film listings

The database at http://www.disabilityfilms.co.uk is huge; its list has  well over 2,000 feature films. Any film that has disability as a major or minor theme seems to have made it onto this labor of love from David Greenhalgh, who provides some annotation and lists of "recommended" films as well.

The NYU Medical Humanities database has a fairly long listing of movies. Go to http://endeavor.med.nyu.edu/lit-med/lit-med-db/keywords.html and search on "disability" for a long list of movies. This has a bit of annotation but there's not much in the way of guidance as  to whether the film would be good of bad for Awareness Day discussion.

Syracuse University's Center on Human Policy offers a shorter but annotated list at http://thechp.syr.edu/Disability_Studies_2003_current.html#Films

Our advice: Always, always, always screen any movie well in advance, and discuss it with your escorts. How will it be used for an Awareness Day discussion? Any film, good or bad, can be fruitful fodder for "awareness." It all depends on how it's presented, and the content of the discussion after the viewing.

**Remember to obtain captioned films — open captioning is best.**

# Appendix D: Short readings

## A Ticket to Bias

### By Susan M. LoTempio

*Susan LoTempio is an assistant managing editor at The Buffalo News. This opinion article originally ran in the Oct. 7, 2005 New York Times and is reprinted with permission from the author. Online at http://www.nytimes.com/2005/10/07/opinion/07lotempio.html*

Buffalo — I was 15 when I first saw the Beatles in concert. That was 1965, long before the Americans with Disabilities Act, so wheelchair seating was rather unpredictable. Lucky for me, the ushers at Toronto's Maple Leaf Gardens pointed me to the front of the arena and told me to stay there.

"There" was right under Paul McCartney's amplifier. A perfect place to be.

"There" last Friday night at Madison Square Garden, 40 years later, was third row on the floor, a few feet away not just from his amplifier, but from Sir Paul himself. An opening night dream seat, you might assume.

Actually, it was a seat from hell.

The ticket was a Mother's Day gift from my 20-year-old daughter. She and my niece scraped together $278, contacted the Garden's disabled services office, and gave me the best gift I've ever received.

Like the thousands of others there that night, I expected a great show, and a great memory.

At the Garden, though, as I was being shown to my seat (a spot at the end of the aisle where a chair had been removed), I wondered if I would be able to see the stage if the fans in front stood up during the show.

Don't worry, the security guards assured me, they know how to handle the situation. I also asked a representative from the Garden's disabled services office. He said the same thing.

When Sir Paul came out and launched into his first number, everyone stood up, and all I could see was a wall of gyrating backsides.

Too close to the stage to even see the huge monitors overhead, I moved into the aisle to try to get a view. The security guard told me to move back. I asked him where I could go to see around the masses of bodies, and he ordered me to stay where I was.

I tried to remain polite, but that painful sensation I get when I'm being dismissed or patronized swept through me and I yelled back, "These tickets cost $300, and I can't see anything."

"Stay there," the security guard shouted, his face just inches from mine. "If you don't like it, you can leave."

He abruptly took off, returning with the guy from the disabled services office, who looked around and said there wasn't much he could do.

It was then that I snapped. More than forty years of having to enter restaurants through kitchen doors; years and years of being carried up the steps of public schools; and countless times being hauled onto airplanes like a baby in a buggy culminated in this one degrading moment. Who gave them the right to take my money and then take away the concert? Who gave them the right to make me look as if I had done something wrong?

And so I left the concert before the former Beatle had even begun his third song.

Yes, someone did ask if I wanted to move to a seat up in the stands. I declined. Was there any other person at that concert - disabled or not - who would sit in the $100 section if her ticket had cost nearly $300? And yes, they did ultimately refund the ticket - but I wanted to see the show more than I wanted the money.

When I asked the Garden staff how they could, in good conscience, sell a ticket that afforded no possible view of the stage for a person who cannot stand up, their response was, "It's an old building."

What about the Americans with Disabilities Act and sight-line regulations, I asked them. Aren't you breaking the law? Again the reply, "It's an old building."

The final blow was when someone from the disabled services office accused me of swapping my ticket to, I suppose, get closer to the stage.

Later, I wondered what Sir Paul would say if he knew what had happened. His wife, after all, is disabled, and maybe she knows what I now know: No matter who you are, no matter how much money you have, no matter how many laws are passed, true equality remains a dream out of reach.

## The Bargain

*The following item is from the Sept./Oct.1989 issue of The Disability Rag, and can be found online at http://www.raggededgemagazine.com/bargain.html*

"This is a revolt against a system based on the assumption that deaf people have to become like hearing people, and have to fit into the dominant hearing society."

The speaker was from DeafPride!, a Washington, D.C.-based organization whose purpose is pretty clear from its name. The occasion was the protest at Gallaudet University which culminated in the first-ever appointment of a deaf president.

For a few brief days in March, 1988, it seems the entire world understood the "revolt" the speaker referred to. What remains of that knowledge a year later? What's happened to the "revolt"? What's happened to that pride?

The speaker that March day was deaf. But others with disabilities echo her belief that we indeed live in a system based on the assumption that disabled people — whatever the disability — have to become like non-disabled "normal" people — or at least keep striving to be "normal" — in order to be essentially OK. "Overcoming their handicaps" is what it's called' it's the basis of our culture's "bargain" with those who incur disability.

Paul Longmore, a  historian of the disability rights movement, outlines The Bargain this way:

"The non-handicapped majority says, in effect, 'we will extend to you provisional and partial toleration of your public presence - as long as you display a continuous cheerful striving toward "normalization."

" 'Cheerful' is the key word here," Longmore points out. Disabled people can't complain, can't whimper — and certainly can't protest. That's not part of The Bargain.

Franklin Delano Roosevelt struck this bargain with society, says Longmore, and "succeeded in selling it as a new image of disability to the American public." It became "the preferred, even the required" image, he says.

This bargain could only be struck in a society that viewed disability as a transgression, something the disabled person could, with effort, "manage" and control — "a private, emotional or physical tragedy best dealt with by psychological coping," Longmore says. This view of disability has-been called the "medical model": it sees the disability itself as the problem, to be dealt with in private, something between doctor and patient.

What price do we as disabled people pay for agreeing to The Bargain? Quite a bit — including our pride.

"The Bargain," Longmore points out, "disallows any collective protest against things like prejudice or discrimination.

"At most," he says, "it permits an effort to 'educate' about 'attitudinal barriers,'" a phrase Longmore considers a euphemism. ("We use a lot of euphemisms," Longmore notes; "we're allowed to call them 'attitudinal barriers' but never outright 'prejudice' or 'discrimination.' That's part of The Bargain too, he says.)

The Bargain FDR struck with society has been forced on three generations of disabled people, says Longmore. Society likes The Bargain because it fits so nicely with the medical model of disability, which was firmly ensconced in our culture at the time FDR encountered polio. The Bargain gives disabled people something "useful" to do: get rehabilitated; strive to be normal.

## A moral problem

Society has not always seen disability as a medical problem. Until a few centuries ago, the presence of disability was considered a moral problem, says Longmore. Though disabled people, it seems, were always exploited and oppressed, political scientist Harlan Hahn says history suggests that in many societies "the physical differences represented by disabilities have also been perceived as socially and sexually desirable."

Hahn ventures that people with deformities in medieval society were regarded as highly erotic — so erotic that the Church sought to control the sensuality disability engendered by promoting images of sterile, "proper" sexuality within marriage and between "normal" people.

It's only been since the eighteenth century or so — roughly from the time of the Enlightenment — that western society has chosen to see disability as an sickness to be treated and disabled people as "problem cases" to be made to conform to the normal majority. Today society is fixated on cure as the salvation of disabled people.

Fear and loathing in the western world

During the last century, fear that "the feebleminded, the mute and deranged" would breed and propagate more of their deviant culture if allowed to mix spawned efforts to keep people with disabilities isolated from each other or institutionalized and restrained from "breeding." Society needed to protect itself from what was called the "neuropathological family," says Longmore.

Deaf people were forcibly prevented from using sign language by teachers in schools for deaf children, and punished severely for infractions.

By the 1930s, over half the states had adopted sterilization laws on people with some disabilities, says Longmore: during the 1930s in Germany, tens of thousands of people with disabilities were put to death in hospitals by those who became the Nazi doctors, perfecting through these killings techniques that would later be used in concentration camps.

It was into such a time that Roosevelt came with his polio.

'Passing for white'

"We never thought of the president as handicapped," said a Roosevelt family friend quoted by Hugh Gallagher in his book "FDR'S Splendid Deception." "We never thought of it at all."

Like many successful "overcomers," people who "just happen to have a disability" but who are not seen as "handicapped," Roosevelt had managed to cross the line separating "normal people" from those society considered deviant and had labeled "the handicapped." Roosevelt had struck The Bargain society needed, so he was considered OK by society. He was, after all, trying to be "normal."

Countless of us with disabilities strike the same implicit bargain with society today.

It's this bargain that has given rise to the countless "help the handicapped" programs of government and private charity. programs whose implicit goal is to help make disabled people more like normal people; that help disabled people "pass for white."

The idea of disabled people being proud of their disability — like DeafPride so obviously is — is antithetical to what such groups stand for. Disabled people in society are afforded grudging acceptance and assimilation only to the extent that they show good-faith efforts at becoming "normal."

The Bargain doesn't allow for protest at injustice. Protest would suggest that disabled people believe they have rights as disabled people. According to The Bargain, a disabled person achieves validity only to the extent she attempts to become normal. If one flaunts one's disability, if one flouts normalcy, one has no right to decent treatment.

The disability rights movement exposes The Bargain for what it is: a way of controlling a minority by forcing upon them the physical standards of the majority culture. It is this which the DeafPride! speaker was rejecting. This is what the disability rights movement rejects. It is society which must change, says the movement; not the individual with the disability. The individual with the disability is alright, disability and all.

This idea, though, still seems radical decades after it was first advanced by people who picked up the 1960's civil rights philosophies of other movements and applied it to their own situation, and saw that fit. Why has the idea not taken the country's disabled minority by storm? Why are so many of us with disabilities still so hesitant when it comes to rights?

Harlan Hahn's been exploring this question, too. In his article, "Can Disability Be Beautiful?" in the Winter, 1988 issue of Social Policy Magazine, he gave what may still be the best explanation.

"Unlike other minorities," he wrote, "disabled men and women have not yet been able to refute" accusations of "biological inferiority." Part of the problem, he believes, is that disabled people have been raised by non-disabled parents in a non-disabled environment, and thus have no sense of a shared culture. Deaf people who sign — particularly deaf people whose parents and relatives are deaf — are among the few groups of disabled people who have a real culture. Many of those people go to Gallaudet; that's why "revolt" occurred among deaf students: they have that sense of community and pride that gave them the strength to challenge the System, that sense of community and pride other, isolated disabled people lack.

Disabled people, says Hahn, lack what he calls a "sense of generational continuity." This generational continuity," he thinks, would "allow the legacy of their experience to become an important solace in an uncaring and inhospitable world."

Hahn believes the roots of discrimination and prejudice against disabled people are grounded in what he calls "aesthetic anxiety - the fear of others whose traits are perceived a disturbing or unpleasant." He thinks this is behind a lot of employment discrimination, for example - and he thinks that if disabled people would acknowledge they're being discriminated against because of these kinds of fears, we'd get further as a civil rights movement.

But, says Hahn, "many persons with disabilities have been reluctant to acknowledge" such discrimination. We don't want people to think we're considered weird or ugly, in other words — so even if that's why we're denied jobs, or a seat in a restaurant - we try to brush off the discrimination. We try to "pass." We've internalized the stigma.

This, of course, is exactly what The Bargain is all about. We're supposed to feel we're the ones in the wrong; the ones who have to "overcome."

True power

Hahn says people with disabilities will find true power as a group only when we acquire self esteem as disabled people — something The Rag refers to Disability Cool. And he believes a reading of history prior to the Enlightenment can give us a way to recapture a pride in what he calls "individuality."

"By reclaiming an aesthetic tradition that originated in one the earliest eras of human history, and by overturning the moral order of the human body imposed by such authorities as the church and the mass media, it is possible to assert proudly that 'disability is beautiful,' " he writes.

The ability to say "disability is beautiful" has "profound social, political and aesthetic implications for non-disabled as well as disabled people," Hahn believes.

When disabled people feel genuinely proud of who they are, they can "play a significant role as critics of a culture that places inordinate stress on a rather conformist vision" of what is aesthetically pleasing. We are capable, as disabled people, of offering to the world "an alternative model of attraction that would permit both disabled and non-disabled persons to discover enhanced aesthetic satisfaction" in all kinds ordinary people — "beautiful" or not.

The majority's rather tired and puritanical ideas of "beauty" could go right out the window, Hahn thinks, if disabled people would feel their own power — and project it onto society, rather than accepting society's projections of stigma as we do now.

But to do this, disabled people must reclaim their history. We must break our side of The Bargain. We must revolt.

Will it happen?

## Social Security Sued for Failing to Accommodate Blind Beneficiaries

*The following item was posted to Ragged Edge Online's News Dept. on Nov. 21, 2005. It can be found online at*
*http://www.raggededgemagazine.com/departments/news/000629.html*

The Social Security Administration, the one federal agency "that should know more about disability than any other," nonetheless continues to send critical information to beneficiaries in print only, even when it knows them to be blind or vision-impaired, says the attorney for the Disability Rights Education and Defense Fund.

Saying they lost benefits when they failed to get critical information in an accessible format and as a result, did not respond to the SSA, a group of blind individuals sued the SSA last week under the Americans with Disabilities Act. The American Council of the Blind has also joined the suit. According to papers filed in the suit, over 100,000 blind and visually impaired people get Social Security benefits. Yet the SSA has not done anything to provide its information via email, which blind people have requested. Arlene Mayerson, the DREDF attorney handling the case, told reporters the only "accommodation" SSA had made was to offer to read benefits documents over the phone, but said the service was sporadic and poorly publicized — and unsuitable to reading complex documents.

The press release from DREDF can be found at
http://www.dredf.org/press_releases/ssa.html

## The New Refugees

### By MaryFrances Platt

*The late MaryFrances Platt, who called herself ""a drooling, plugged-in, wheeling, broke-down, radical crip," wrote frequently for Ragged Edge. This article was originally published in the March/April 2003 issue of Ragged Edge magazine. It can be found online at http://www.raggededgemagazine.com/0303/0303ft4.html*

I can often be found spending large spaces and places of time on the road, living in my van. I am a Girl Scout and outdoor education leader from way back, but my frequent camping forays are really about my heart and lungs requiring me to be a snowbird following the warmth, and about my MCS requiring me to be in a non-toxic environment.

My own home, which I have taken great lengths to make safe for myself, can easily make me ill in the winter with closed windows and less opportunity for clean air exchange, and more opportunity for perfumed personal care attendants and neighbors to send me into respiratory arrest with their hairspray or clothes detergent. Many years ago, a healer that I trust greatly told me that I simply could not live in a climate where the windows could not stay open. She was right. So every winter, off I go to warmer climates as my lease, health, and mobility allow.

Those of you who have attended ADAPT actions and other events that I have been present at know that I don't stay in hotels, but rather lay my body down in the back of my van. I do this no matter what the climate. Living with MCS, I can't just leave a cold-ridden toxic environment and find a nice cheap hotel or temporary apartment in a warmer climate. The normal scents and chemicals in your average hotel would render me extremely ill with respiratory and neurological symptoms.

❋ ❋ ❋

Folks like me, with multiple chemical sensitivity, sometimes call ourselves the "new refugees." You'll find us moving from place to place, hoping to find somewhere we will not get sick. More often than not, there is no room in any inn that doesn't cause us to wheeze, hurl, whiz, puke, or pass out. And if we do find a place, all it takes is one unknowing or uncaring person using one squirt of some toxic hairspray to set us off and running again, in an MCS reaction, without a safe place to lay our bodies down. If we are lucky, we pack up what we have and set out in our vehicles. For many of us, our vehicles provide the only MCS-safe space available.

My baby-poop-yellow van "Pumpkin" is infamous. She is 18 years old. We have been together for 15 years. In two years she will be eligible for antique plates. It's not that I'm overly good to my vehicles; it's that I have not been able to find any other vehicle that doesn't make me ill.

I bought a newer van in the early '90s, tore out the carpet, cloth walls, and vinyl coverings. Still it made me sick. Today it sits in a yard in New Hampshire, detoxing for the 15-year period it usually takes for something to outgas all its chemical toxicity.

I think I have spent more nights sleeping in Pumpkin than in my apartment of ten years! She is always there for me to run to — or with — as I need.

In my escapes across the country I have come across other MCSers living in their vehicles, trailers, or a combination of canvas and metal. I have found them in federal, state, and private campgrounds, and on so-called public lands that have no facilities at all. Many an MCSer has spent a winter dry-docked in the public lands outside of Tucson. I have been amazed at our ability to keep moving on, and yet I am not surprised when I hear of a new MCS suicide. We eventually reach the end of our ropes, with no place to live, no safe water, no food we can eat without getting sick, and no place to lay our weary heads at night.

Most of the medical establishment doesn't believe we have an illness. Those who believe we do still don't have a clue how to treat us, much less cure us.

I was living in an 8-by-10 metal storage shed for the winter on some "disabled women's land" and feeling a bit crowded until Margaret arrived. Margaret had been living in the same Volkswagen bug for 26 years — and yes, that's "bug" with a "g," not "bus" with an "s." Everything she owned was contained in that teeny tiny space.

Each night she would move everything from the inside of her VW bug, in their 15- and 20-year-old detoxed boxes and bags, to the outside so she could sleep in the bug. Her curtains were old, wrinkled, unscented paper bags. The blanket she used, as well as the clothes she wore, she washed by hand, no detergent.

Margaret loved animals but was allergic to their dander. Most mornings I'd awaken to find my cat sitting about 15 feet away from her, while she cooed at him, and he meowed at her, from a distance. If he moved closer, she'd tell him, "Now Mazel, you know I am allergic to you" — and he would back off. Margaret would pet my assistance dog, Lucy, by means of a long stick.

People were not as understanding as the animals were. Margaret never stayed too long at one spot. She had to be aware of what the water supply was doing in the area, as well as what chemicals were being sprayed where, as barely a sniff would make her very very ill. A migrant MCSer, she had to follow the patterns of the winds and the rains. After two months on the land where I stayed, it was time for her to move on as the pesticide spraying began. Off she went, to some Quaker land for another few months. This was her whole life, and she certainly made the best of it. My animals missed her immensely. =

❀ ❀ ❀

June developed MCS later in life. With her Social Security payments, she had the good sense to buy an old detoxed motor home which she lived in fulltime. The Airstream brand of old motor home is revered by MCSers for its low toxicity, and this is what June had. Many of us are allergic to new wood -or any kind of wood; for us, metal living spaces are imperative. I lived in my 8-by-10 metal storage shed, others lived in their 22-ft. trailers. June had a legitimate permanent address, yet she traveled around the country, staying in the warm western climates and living mostly on public lands.

"Public lands" are lands, generally owned by the National Park Service, that for the most part are legal to camp on. Some have limited stays, some you can stay a long time, some have loopholes that you have to figure out. Most of these type of lands have no facilities and no fees, so many people with MCS find their way to them. They also tend to be less populated — therefore one is exposed less to perfumes and chemicals.

It is best to have a legitimate "carry permit" if you frequent any of these spaces, though, as predators of the human as well as the animal kind tend to find their way there. I still hold a memory of June, one foot in her RV, one on the outside step, shotgun pointed at the figure walking toward her, asking him to "state his business, please!"

June over the years became an MCS activist. Now, after many years on the road, she longs for a stable, MCS-safe community. She has been unsuccessful but relentless in her efforts to organize this community. My guess is that she will succeed someday, but until it happens, she still jumps from one public land to another, as she can not afford campground or trailer park fees living on SSDI.

If one is disabled, and can prove it, one can acquire a pass that allows you to pay half price on national and federal parks. This includes national forests and conservation corps lands, as well as national parks

The depression and isolation one can feel from living with MCS is devastating. When every person you come in contact with may be a potential "germ" or bearer of toxicity, it becomes necessary to just stop connecting.

People with MCS, from necessity, live in incredible isolation. Yet we still manage to keep being independent and keep on keeping on. Sometimes I really don't know how the hell we do it.

People who find out about my disability-generated refugee lifestyle will say, "gee — aren't you afraid to travel, live, be, fill-in-the-blank, alone?"

Of course I am! I tell them. I am a disabled woman traveling alone, camping out in isolated places and everyday campgrounds — of course I am scared! But I am more afraid of not being alive. And if I were to stay at home during the coldest part of the winter, I would die.

My MCS friends are in the same boat. If they remain in a toxic environment, they can die from neurological or respiratory illness.

Right now, very little is being done for people with MCS. Some of us try allergy-type treatments. Others use pain killers. Some of us get some supportive therapies. Mostly, though, even within the disability community, we remain isolated and segregated.

Two years ago, while camping at some national lands, I came across a man who never even told me his name. He appeared to be living out of the back of a truck that had a small camper on it with a homemade canvas awning that extended out almost over his whole site. It included quite an elaborate camp kitchen. The camping land on which I met him allows two-week stays — but you could stay there two weeks, pack up, leave for 24 hours, and then come back; you could do that three times (that is also the regulation for Florida state parks).

I stopped to chat with this gentleman a few times, and soon caught on to the fact that, whatever else he had going on, he also had some psychiatric disabilities. Since a lot of his stuff was camouflage-colored, I ventured to ask if he had been in the service. Yes indeed, he told me; he had been to the Gulf War. He informed me that he "suffered" from post traumatic stress as well as multiple allergies from exposure to unknown chemicals. He found that he could no longer live in houses, he said. He wasn't sure whether it made him sick, crazy, or a combination of both, but he felt better living in his truck, he said. I had a number of conversations with him, and often only a small portion of them could I really decipher, but I did figure out that he probably had MCS, and was affected neurologically by chemical exposure, both then and now.

He was receiving Social Security benefits, and was fighting for Veterans' benefits as well. I can only hope that now that they know about Gulf War Syndrome, he has been appropriately compensated, and is still managing to live his life, somewhere, somehow.

I have met many homeless crips hiding out in national and state parks. Some had MCS, some didn't. All were living in poverty, fleeing one place for another. What we all had in common was our tenacity for living.

❀ ❀ ❀

One of the most painful things that crips with MCS have to deal with is the fact that most people with disabilities exclude us, discriminating against us in their non-air-filtered, carpeted independent living centers filled with crips who have dosed themselves in perfume, disinfectant, hairspray and the like.

The National Council on Independent Living has issued a policy stating that no scents or perfumes be worn at meetings. But just last week I spoke to an independent living center director, reminding her not to lay carpet in the new center being planned. They had planned on having one room remain uncarpeted, she told me. It would have a separate entrance.

I had to point out to her that in that case, folks with MCS would still not be able to work there.

This interaction is indicative of where disability rights appears to be regarding MCS access and reality.

My message to those of you involved in independent living centers — and in planning crip events — is this: Please stop excluding us. Please start taking MCS access seriously. Remember: we are the canaries in the mine, alerting others to what may soon be in store for them as well. You too could catch this "disease" just from living in the toxic environment of the 21st century.

The next time you make the decision to put down "sick-making" carpeting in your office, remember: the next person it could be making sick — and segregating — is you.

## 'I Don't Consider Myself Disabled'

By Mary Johnson

*Mary Johnson is the editor of Ragged Edge Online, and author of Make Them Go Away: Clint Eastwood, Christopher Reeve & The Case Against Disability Rights (Advocado Press, 2003) from which this excerpt is taken.*

Haven't you heard someone say, "Oh, I don't consider myself disabled"? How many times have you said it yourself about someone? It's meant as a compliment. What does that mean? That to say someone is disabled is in a way an insult — saying something bad about them. It can't be otherwise.

Disability advocates have known this, at least on an instinctive level, for a long time; it's the real reason behind the push toward what they call "people first" language — and it's why the Americans with Disabilities Act is called that, rather than, for example, the Disabled Americans Act. (Great Britain's similar law, passed in 1995, is more appropriately called The Disability Discrimination Act.) It's the reason behind the increasingly silly constructions of "people with" that get mocked so regularly: "people with vision impairments," "people with autism," "people with cerebral palsy," "people with spinal cord injuries." Advocates of "people first" constructions say it is important to realize that the person is not "disabled" but rather that they "have" a disability.

This and a lot of other psychological and linguistic gyrations can't hide the fact that to be disabled is to be considered something bad. When John Stossel on his TV special The Blame Game told us admiringly that Marc Simitian "doesn't consider himself a victim," he was making the same point.

"Don't call me disabled," Nick Ackerman told reporters. The Iowa college senior, who had used prosthetic legs since an accident in early childhood, who won the NCAA Division 3 wrestling championship, told a reporter that "I don't have a disability, I have ability and I'm going to use it" and that "I always thought I was normal."

An admiring New York Times obituary reported that Celeste Tate Harrington, "a quadriplegic street musician whose buoyant personality and unremitting chutzpah brought astounded smiles to everyone who watched her play the keyboard with her lips and tongue on Atlantic City's Boardwalk," "didn't consider herself disabled." Nana Graham was born with "undeveloped legs and feet that curved inward and upside down." Her legs were amputated when she was 13. But her daughter told a reporter Graham was "not handicapped." Hearing-impaired actress Vanessa Vaughan insisted she was not disabled and refused to be interviewed by the Toronto Star for an article about disabled performers. Wheelchair tennis star Dan Bennett, "born with spina bifida, leaving him without use of his legs," did not consider himself disabled. "The more we play, the more words like 'handicapped' and 'disabled' can begin to disappear," wheelchair tennis player Joe Babakanian told a reporter. . . .

The obituary for Bob L. Thomas, chief justice of the 10th Circuit Court of Appeals in Waco, Tex., noted that he had achieved "success in law and politics despite total paralysis in all but his left hand," having "contracted polio at the age of 15." He used a wheelchair until his death, yet a colleague remarked that he didn't consider himself disabled. "He had an absolute determination to overcome his disabilities," said another.

When Louisvillian Dan Massie died, a story noting his role as a 1970s disability activist reported that although his wife pushed him everywhere in his chair, he "didn't act as if he was disabled." "He didn't take a penny of Social Security disability money," a friend told a reporter. "He sold jewelry on street corners and at festivals, and earned all his money."

If my grandmother has arthritis, but she isn't "really disabled," what we are saying is that she does not have the attributes we believe those poor schmucks "the disabled" have. Or, if we think she does have those attributes, it's a signal she's left the "us" and moved to the "them" category, and we no longer see her as being like us but as being like "the disabled."

Even people who don't have any real luxury of shifting in or out of the "disabled" category — people like Christopher Reeve and John Hockenberry who everyone can tell are clearly disabled — are brought into the "us" camp by the statement that they don't "act disabled." Congresswoman Barbara Jordan, who had multiple sclerosis, did not discuss her disability openly.

People do not want to identify as disabled and will do almost anything to avoid it. If we act normal and don't get involved in that disability rights stuff, then we're not really disabled, we think. If we keep on trying to recover, then, we think, we're not truly disabled. President Roosevelt, even though he could not walk unaided, nevertheless called himself a "cured cripple." It was his way of doing the same thing.

# A Hard Look at Invisible Disability

## By Cal Montgomery

*Cal Montgomery is a frequent contributor to Ragged Edge Online. This article was published in the March/April 2001 issue of Ragged Edge magazine. It can be found online at http://www.raggededgemagazine.com/0301/0301ft1.htm*

I am invisibly disabled — or so I'm told. The problem is that I don't believe a distinction between visible and invisible disability is useful, or even meaningful.

It takes practice, I guess, for other people to understand the ways disability affects my life. Some experience with me, or at least with people who are like me in some way, will give you a much better handle on what I'm going to have trouble with, and why.

In other words, as you come to know me, you'll get better at spotting the barriers I face when I want to participate in the life of my community, my society, my world. You'll learn to spot the strobing fluorescents, to catch the verbal constructions that trip me up, to notice when I cannot recognize the people and objects in front of me and the speech and other sounds around me.

Spend enough time with me and you'll understand not only that I need to have expectations and anticipated events laid out for me, but why. You may be surprised at first that I can manage in one situation and not another, but eventually you'll probably learn to tell the difference.

As I watch wheelchair users' different problems with the same curb cut, I am reminded that it takes practice to really understand how disability affects any individual's life. Every so often I am surprised when someone is stopped short by a curb cut I thought she could navigate. But my failure to see the barrier doesn't make it invisible.

In the disability community, we speak as if some kinds of disability were visible, and others weren't. Let me suggest a different approach: think about the ways different kinds of disability have become more familiar, and more visible, to you as you've gotten to know more disabled people.

When non-disabled people look at "the disabled," they see wheelchairs and picture-boards. They see helmets and hearing aids and white canes. With a few exceptions, they don't pick up on how individuals differ from one another; they notice the tools we use. And these tools, to the general public, equal "disability." Venture out without a well-known tool, and your disability is "invisible" or "hidden."

But the tools are only the first step to visibility. The second step is the behavior that is expected, given a particular set of tools. The person who uses a white cane when getting on the bus, but then pulls out a book to read while riding; the person who uses a wheelchair to get into the library stacks but then stands up to reach a book on a high shelf; the person who uses a picture-board to discuss philosophy; the person who challenges the particular expectations of disability that other people have is suspect. "I can't see what's wrong with him," people say, meaning, "He's not acting the way I think he should." "She's invisibly disabled," they say, meaning, "I can't see what barriers she faces."

Why, you might ask, do I even bring this up within the disability community? Although we may understand disability differently than others do, we have not, as a group, abandoned the suspicion of people who may not be "really" disabled, who may be "slacking" or "faking" or encroaching on "our" movement and "our" successes. And we respond to people who challenge our ideas of what disabled people are "really like" just as non-disabled people do: with suspicion.

We also have developed a fixed idea of what "accessible" means, and when "invisibly disabled" people complain of barriers we can't pick out, it's too easy to dismiss them as unimportant distractions from the "real" issues — the issues that "visibly disabled" people are concerned with. After all, the "visible" barriers cannot be ignored.

But a meeting in a room with a ramped entrance isn't accessible to everyone if the meeting is held in a language not everyone understands. It isn't accessible to everyone if the rules are complicated enough that not everyone who wants to participate can figure out how to do so. It isn't accessible to everyone if the information that will be discussed wasn't available in forms that everyone could understand.

Because "the invisibly disabled," like all who defy expectation, are suspect, people ask us why we need accommodation rather than what accommodation we need. "What seems to be the problem?" they ask, when we point out barriers. "Everyone else can do it," they assure us. "It's already accessible." And while, for example, wheelchair users no longer accept being carried up a flight of stairs "as a favor," we are too often expected to smile gratefully and accept favors instead of rights.

It goes beyond that, though. Even other disabled people who rankle at the question, "What's wrong with you?" will turn and ask me the same question — and expect a detailed and deferential answer. Even other disabled people, when faced with an accommodation request they regard as strange (for a disability they regard as invisible), defend barriers. "You have to understand," they say as we struggle for access. "You have to be patient."

And to that I respond, "Why should some disabled people get to demand justice now, while others are expected to be patient and understanding in the face of injustice?" Why should some people's reasonable accommodation requests be treated as assertions about disabling barriers and others' merely as statements of personal preference?

Every person is unique — though the defenders of the non-disabled status quo would like to believe we are all the same. Even within the disability community, we vary: we have different things we cannot do, or do as long as or as well as or in the same way as non-disabled people. And this means our experience of disability varies: different aspects of the way society has arranged things are barriers to different people.

We will always need to learn from one another about the barriers each of us faces, and barrier removal will need to be an ongoing process, not an accomplishment we can safely put behind us. Dismissing that which is unfamiliar to us as "invisible" (and suggesting that it cannot be discerned rather than that we have not learned to discern it) is another way of throwing the responsibility for social justice back on the individual who carries the burden of injustice.

I am invisibly disabled — or so I'm told. That means my access is my problem.
I disagree.

The disability rights movement is based on the conviction that varying from one another doesn't mean we have to face ableism, to deal with environments and interactions that are designed for some — and not all — of humanity, to experience the injustice of being left out because there is something we cannot do.

So let me challenge all of us: among ourselves, let's give up belief in "invisible disability." Let's work as a cross-disability community in a way that acknowledges all disabled people — all people — as individuals. Let's agree that no-one should face ableism either inside or outside the disability community, and let's act on that agreement.

## Sports Websites Mostly Inaccessible to Blind Superbowl Fans

*The following item was posted to Ragged Edge Online's News Dept. on Feb. 2, 2006. It can be found online at http://www.raggededgemagazine.com/departments/news/000777.html*

Just in time for Super Bowl XL, The American Foundation for the Blind has released a report that finds major sports websites that Superbowl fans are logging into to check stats and read up on the players to be — surprise! — pretty much inaccessible to blind sports fans.

The group checked out NFL.com, ESPN.com and SI.com using Window-Eyes 5.5, a popular screen reader. "All three sites are very cluttered, and have several design problems that make them difficult to navigate with a screen reader," says the AFB. ESPN.com was the worst, said the group.

NFL.com's home page is "vastly complex with almost 200 links" — and though they're labeled, there are no headings. And "signing up for Field Pass—which allows users to watch games live, tune in to official home team radio announcers, and access pre- and post-game coverage—" is impossible for users of screen-reading browsers. "The user is immediately confronted by two inaccessible links."

But visitors to ESPN.com are immediately confronted with five indecipherable links, says the Foundation. And the site is full of what the Foundation describes as "improperly coded Flash content."

Read the full report on the website of the American Foundation for the Blind at http://www.afb.org/Section.asp?SectionID=57&DocumentID=3021

## Deaf Hunger Striker Protesting Lack of ASL at Michigan School for Deaf

*The following item was posted to Ragged Edge Online's World-O-Blogs Dept. on Nov. 28, 2005. It can be found online at*
*http://www.raggededgemagazine.com/departments/worldoblogs/000644.html*

As we post this on Monday, Nov. 28, a former instructor at the Michigan School for the Deaf is in the 8th day of his hunger strike. Ryan Commerson's individual act of protest against a school that he says refuses to offer bilingual education in American Sign Language as well as English is drawing attention from around the country. Commerson's protest, which has widespread student support, is also calling for the hiring of a deaf principal and employing staff members who are fluent American Sign Language.

From the Flint (MI) Journal:

> On Monday, 43 out of 160 MSD students were suspended for leaving school to join Commerson, 30. The suspensions end next week.

> There also was a fight between some parents coming to pick up their suspended students from school Monday, but there were no serious injuries.

The blog at http://starvingforaccess.blog.com has been started to chronicle the protest and to garner support for the reforms Commerson is calling for.

From the blog:

> Ryan continues to sit in outside all day. He still has not eaten and has lost 15 pounds to date.

> Today was warmer than the last few days, but it rained. Tomorrow, there will be a meeting with Jeremy Hughes, from the Department of Education. John Austin, the Vice President of the State Board of Education has been a huge assistance in arranging the meeting. We are grateful to him for all of his hard work through the holidays.

> Ryan reports struggling with extreme hunger pains that are more intense and frequent. He is very tempted to eat, but has not done so. He is so tired....

# The Americans with Disabilities Act Findings

**The following "findings and purposes" lays out the reasons Congress listed for passing the Americans with Disabilities Act of 1990 (Public Law 101-336). This is taken from Section 2 of the Act, 42 U.S.C. §12101. The text of the Americans with Disabilities Act can be found online at http://www.usdoj.gov/crt/ada/pubs/ada.txt**

AMERICANS WITH DISABILITIES ACT of 1990
SEC. 2. FINDINGS AND PURPOSES.
(a) Findings.—The Congress finds that—

(1) some 43,000,000 Americans have one or more physical or mental disabilities, and this number is increasing as the population as a whole is growing older;

(2) historically, society has tended to isolate and segregate individuals with disabilities, and, despite some improvements, such forms of discrimination against individuals with disabilities continue to be a serious and pervasive social problem;

(3) discrimination against individuals with disabilities persists in such critical areas as employment, housing, public accommodations, education, transportation, communication, recreation, institutionalization, health services, voting, and access to public services;

(4) unlike individuals who have experienced discrimination on the basis of race, color, sex, national origin, religion, or age, individuals who have experienced discrimination on the basis of disability have often had no legal recourse to redress such discrimination;

(5) individuals with disabilities continually encounter various forms of discrimination, including outright intentional exclusion, the discriminatory effects of architectural, transportation, and communication barriers, overprotective rules and policies, failure to make modifications to existing facilities and practices, exclusionary qualification standards and criteria, segregation, and relegation to lesser services, programs, activities, benefits, jobs, or other opportunities;

(6) census data, national polls, and other studies have documented that people with disabilities, as a group, occupy an inferior status in our society, and are severely disadvantaged socially, vocationally, economically, and educationally;

(7) individuals with disabilities are a discrete and insular minority who have been faced with restrictions and limitations, subjected to a history of purposeful unequal treatment, and relegated to a position of political powerlessness in our society, based on characteristics that are beyond the control of such individuals and resulting from stereotypic assumptions not truly indicative of the individual ability of such individuals to participate in, and contribute to, society;

(8) the Nation's proper goals regarding individuals with disabilities are to assure equality of opportunity, full participation, independent living, and economic self-sufficiency for such individuals; and

(9) the continuing existence of unfair and unnecessary discrimination and prejudice denies people with disabilities the opportunity to compete on an equal basis and to pursue those opportunities for which our free society is justifiably famous, and costs the United States billions of dollars in unnecessary expenses resulting from dependency and nonproductivity.

(b) Purpose.—It is the purpose of this Act—

(1) to provide a clear and comprehensive national mandate for the elimination of discrimination against individuals with disabilities;

(2) to provide clear, strong, consistent, enforceable standards addressing discrimination against individuals with disabilities;

(3) to ensure that the Federal Government plays a central role in enforcing the standards established in this Act on behalf of individuals with disabilities; and

(4) to invoke the sweep of congressional authority, including the power to enforce the fourteenth amendment and to regulate commerce, in order to address the major areas of discrimination faced day-to-day by people with disabilities.

Find this text online at http://www.usdoj.gov/crt/ada/pubs/ada.txt

# Appendix E:
# Articles about disability simulations from Ragged Edge

## The Wrong Message

By Valerie Brew-Parrish

*Valerie Brew-Parrish is a polio survivor and longtime disability activist. She writes a column on disability issues for the Joliet, IL Herald News. This article was originally published in the March/April 1997 issue of Ragged Edge magazine. It can be found online at http://www.raggededgemagazine.com/archive/aware.htm*

Hey, Hey, Hey, it's Disability Awareness Day! Everyone gets a chance to see what it's really like to have a disability! Yank out those blindfolds, grab cotton to stuff in your ears, and plop yourself in a wheelchair to navigate around an obstacle course! To get the most out of Disability Awareness Day, it is important to try almost all the disabilities on for size.

Now it is time to tie one of your arms behind you so you can fully appreciate a paralyzed limb.

No doubt about it, life with a disability is a tragedy! Why these poor gimps, blinks, and others would be better off dead! They are so courageous and yet pitiful as they go about their daily routines. Yep, I'm so glad it is their fate and not mine . . .

Sadly, these are the misconceptions that the public holds about those of us who live with disabilities. Disability simulations do nothing but reinforce these negative stereotypes about persons with disabilities.

Like the Jerry Lewis Telethon, disability simulations should be abolished. The disability community should be as outraged by disability simulations as they are over the negative implications of telethons. Overwhelming feelings of pity well up in those who simulate a disability — and pity does not equate with dignity. Disability simulations rob persons with disabilities of their dignity and self respect.

Simulations are phony. To "simulate" means to assume the mere appearance of — without the reality. The reality is this: non-disabled persons can never understand what it is like to have a disability. Jumping in a wheelchair for a few minutes, wearing a blindfold, and stuffing cotton in one's ears does not make a person understand life with a disability.

People who have never been disabled who simulate a disability are often terrified. Many of the "simulators" even cheat a little. Haven't we all observed a person standing up in their wheelchair in order to lift the chair over a curb? They breathe a collective sigh of relief knowing full well that their charade will soon come to an end and their momentary disability will gratefully vanish.

Agencies purportedly serving disabled clients frequently advocate disability simulations, with fancy brochures encouraging the public to assume a disability with blindfolds and wheelchairs. The pamphlets gleefully expound the theory that disability simulations are useful for teaching family members and others what the person with a disability is really experiencing.

What these rehab professionals fail to realize is that the public does not have the coping skills or strategies developed by people who actually have disabilities.

This point was clearly illustrated a few years ago when airline personnel decided to blindfold themselves to test evacuation procedures in case of an airline crash. The results were disastrous. Naturally. The airline staff had no training in mobility or orientation. Therefore, they erroneously concluded that blind persons could never safely evacuate a plane. Nothing could be further from the truth.

When I'm disoriented in a dark place, I let my blind husband lead the way! The National Federation of the Blind has long argued that disability simulations are destructive. Other disability groups should follow their lead and speak out against these sordid attempts to empathize with us by becoming gimp for a day.

For several years, I was employed at a large university that sponsored an annual "Disability Awareness Day." Despite protests from students and staff with disabilities, the non-disabled sponsors of the event continued the spectacle.

I was told by participants that I was an inspiration because I coped so well with my disability. Others told me they would rather be dead than live with a disabling condition. The participants of the simulation debacle now looked at me with pity. In their eyes, I was no longer on an equal basis with them; they felt superior because all of their limbs were in proper working condition.

Regrettably, it seems every annual celebration of the passage of the Americans with Disabilities Act, every disability awareness event, is combined with a tasteless display of disability simulations. In many instances, persons with disabilities are actually participating and perpetuating these contemptible attempts to make the public aware.

Awareness Days can be beneficial if it they are done properly; it is important for the public to meet with persons with disabilities and to interact with us. Why not have people who use wheelchairs discuss obstacles and the need for accessibility? Deaf persons can demonstrate sign language skills, and blind persons can show proper travel techniques. The public needs to know we exist; that we are professionals, parents and homeowners just like them.

But disability simulations need to die a quick death. There are more effective and positive ways to educate the public. Come on folks, we can do a better job getting our messages across. We do not need people to pretend they have disabilities and simulate our disabilities to understand us. All of us need to demand to be treated with dignity. When disability simulations become extinct, perhaps the flood of pity will dry up and be replaced with respect.

## Awareness Days: Some Alternatives to Simulation Exercises

By Prof. Art Blaser

*Prof. Blaser chairs the Political Science Dept. at Chapman University. This article was originally published in the Sept./Oct. 2003 issue of Ragged Edge magazine. It can be found online at http://www.raggededgemagazine.com/0903/0903ft1.html*

1. Talk about doing simulations — without doing them. What are the kinds of experiences that only a non-disabled person simulating a disabled one would have? What are simulations designed to do? Is that a desirable objective? Do they really accomplish that objective? Why, or why not?

2. Listen to a disabled person — one in your neighborhood, your class, around school Ask them about their life — not about medical aspects of the disability. When we compare what we've found out, we'll have heard not from a couple of "experts" but from enough people to realize that there are differences and similarities. Then compare the findings with information about disabled people in the U.S. from the U.S. Census and Harris surveys done for the National Organization on Disability.

3. Read a book or watch a video about a person with a disability. John Hockenberry's Moving Violations is a good book; When Billy Broke his Head is a good video, so is Kiss My Wheels. Consider whether the experiences depicted are typical or atypical and why.

4. Try not doing something: If a restaurant isn't accessible, try not going there. If a restroom isn't accessible, don't use it. If there's space to do so, see a movie from the "wheelchair section." If you go with friends, don't suggest or restrict where they sit.

5. Some people with disabilities insist that there are many positive aspects to the experience of being disabled. Discuss why they say this.

6. Survey neighborhoods: cars parked over driveways, unleashed dogs, sidewalks and curb-cuts, color contrast on stairs ( people with low vision need this), branches that can hit a blind person. Note audible cues (such as horns honking).

   ☛ Find a curb cut. Is the "cut" flush with the street at the bottom, or is there still a lip? Is the curb cut broken? Would it be easy or hard to use it in a wheelchair? Are cars parked in front of it, making it unusable?

   ☛ Look at the entrance to your favorite coffee shop or bookstore. Is it flat? Is there a small step? Are there lots of steps? What would need to be altered to make it accessible? Sometimes there's a loading ramp in back a disabled person can use. What do you think about having to enter that way?

☛ Go to a local clothing shop in the mall. Notice how much space there is between racks of clothes. What would this be like for someone who is blind or who has a mobility disability?

7. Find out what confronts a family traveling and living in motels or hotels. Visit a local hotel. Find out where TDD/TTY phones are and how you would find one if you were deaf. Find out what choices you'd have if you needed to get a wheelchair accessible room for a family of 6. If you were a wheelchair user, would you be able to use the bathroom in the room? Or the shower?

8. Search for a personal assistant. Find out what the job entails. Local newspapers will contain ads. The local center for independent living is a source of other leads. Some people work through companies listed in the Yellow Pages. Without misrepresenting yourself, find out what they charge and what they pay. Would you take such a job? Why or why not?

9. Doing the things above may reinforce your idea of just of how bad it is being disabled.. Using a 5 x 8 card, anonymously write down reactions you'd have if you were to wake up as a member of the other gender. How would you react? How would your family, your friends and your neighbors react? Now share this with the others in your group doing this exercise. Did it turn out that a lot of your preconceptions were just plain silly?

10. Even obviously artificial pretending can be lots of fun. There are three exercises you may want to do. Try these at home:

☛ Bob Cummings, who used to be executive director of the Center for Independent Living in Orange Co., CA., would ask his audiences to shut their eyes. He'd then ask if they'd stopped thinking about their next meal, their appointments with friends, or what they'd be doing an hour from now. Of course they hadn't! His point was that an awful lot remains the same whether you are blind (as he was) or not. The example he liked to give of what he couldn't do was skeet shooting — which he'd never done (nor had any desire to do) before he was blind, either.

☛ "Stuffing your mouths with marshmallows will produce speech like mine," Blaser tells his students. "Does that then mean you will then know how I think, too? If so, then I can go home. You could, too, but you wouldn't do well in the class."

☛ A simulation with practical effect is the closed fist that can't open round door hardware, but can open lever type door handles. The open hand will open either type.

In the exercises above, some disabilities are covered more than others. Why might that be?

## Official 'Awareness': When simulations work

By Ed Eames

*Ed Eames chairs the Fresno, CA ADA Advisory Council. This article was originally posted to Ragged Edge Online on Dec. 11, 2003. It can be found online at http://www.ragged-edgemagazine.com/extra/eamesawareday1103.html*

As part of the blind community, I have been opposed to disability simulation exercises, believing they lead more to fear than to enlightenment. However, other members of the Fresno ADA Advisory Council, a cross-disability group working with city government agencies, persuaded me to go along with their desire to inaugurate the first Disability Awareness Day on October 15, 2003 with disability simulation activities for city officials.

The results were astounding.

Members of the City Council, the County Board of Supervisors and top administrators were invited to take part, and 15 wheelchairs were borrowed from a local provider for the officials to use for a day. The date selected, October 15, is White Cane/Guide Dog Safety Day, and symbolized the cross-disability nature of the event.

Each non-disabled wheelchair user was paired with a real disabled wheelchair user and a nonwheelchair using volunteer. After some short speeches at City Hall, the fifteen participants were given their assignments and sent on their way. For the next hour and a half they rolled around the streets in the downtown Fresno area.

Here are some of the results:

☛ A City Council member almost fell out of his chair while going down an improperly constructed sidewalk ramp. After going through mud-lined streets, he needed lots of Handi Wipes to get himself clean!

☛ The head of the Fresno transportation system was never picked up at the bus stop where he waited for more than 40 minutes. Rolling down one curb, he almost got immobilized when caught between the down curb and uplifted asphalt in the street. He is now arranging for all of his top administrative personnel to go through a similar exercise.

* A Board of Supervisors member was asked to leave the lobby of an office building; she and other wheelchair users were accused of interfering with a postal worker's ability to deliver the mail! The request was made by an irate attorney whose office was located in the building, and astounded the supervisor. This encounter opened the way to discussing the prevalence of attitudinal as well as physical barriers.

☛ The director of the Department of Public Works (which oversees the installation of curb cuts/ramps) was very unhappy with a couple of the cuts he had to traverse to get to the lunch venue.

☛ Several members of the California Department of Transportation became aware of the significance of curb cuts as they wheeled about the area. The ADA Council is negotiating with CalTrans to put curb ramps in on state-controlled overpasses on Route 99 as it goes through the city; now, we think, we are more likely to get them in the immediate future than we might have had this exercise not taken place.

More than 75 individuals showed up at lunch in the nearby state building, and the ersatz wheelchair users shared some of their experiences with the audience. Lots of verbal commitments to support the ADA Council's efforts were made. Now it is up to us to translate these promises into reality!

The biggest disappointment of the day was the lack of publicity. Unfortunately, just two weeks before the event, we learned that President Bush would be in town that day for a fundraiser. He got all the media coverage and raised a couple of million dollars for his campaign! Next year we'll have to check with the Bush campaign to determine when he will be in town!

## The Wrong Message — Still

By Valerie Brew-Parrish

*Valerie Brew-Parrish is a polio survivor and longtime disability activist. She writes a column on disability issues for the Joliet, IL Herald News. This article was originally published in August, 2004 on the Ragged Edge Online website. It can be found online at http://www.raggededgemagazine.com/focus/wrongmessage04.html*

HEY, HEY, HEY it's Disability Awareness Day! Still. Even in the 21st century!

Schools, government agencies, and sometimes, deplorably, gimp groups, are still offering the public "try on a disability" programs — exercises in which non-disabled people are blindfolded, put into wheelchairs or given earplugs to "simulate" having a disability.

When I first wrote my article, The Wrong Message, back in 1997 for the Ragged Edge, I never imagined the stir it would cause. I am proud that the article has made people think about the harm simulations can do.

I still consider simulations an atrocity perpetuated — mostly — by non-disabled professionals. Disabled folks are sometimes involved though, as well.

I don't know who dreamed up the concept of "disability simulations" but they have been around for a mighty long time. My lifelong friend, Michael A. Winter, now the Director of Civil Rights for the U.S. Department of Transportation, first exposed me to the shameful practice. Michael and I were classmates at a segregated school for crips and met in 6th grade. We attended the same university. As undergrads, Michael formed a group called Wheelchair Action. When the Rehabilitation Institute at Southern Illinois University sponsored a disability simulation, Michael and members of his group stormed into the classroom and tried in vain to halt the fiasco.

Professionals who are non-disabled rarely stop to listen to the people who live with disabilities. I was proud of Michael for trying to get people to understand how destructive these simulations can be.

Non-disabled people usually come away from disability simulations

☛ thinking life is a tragedy for persons with disabilities,

☛ thanking the good Lord they are not saddled with a disability

☛ or falling prey to the "amazing" syndrome: "Ohhhhh just lookie at what disabled people can do! They're better than us at (getting around in the dark, popping wheelies, reading hand signs . . . )"

When I wrote "The Wrong Message," I was angry. My daughter Tara had come home from school in tears. It was Disability Simulation Day at Greenwood High. Blindfolded students were being led around by sighted students, others were bumping into walls. The students were terrified of their newly created disabilities. Some had told Tara they thought persons with disabilities had horrible lives; a few thought they might be better off dead.

School personnel knew that both Tara's parents had disabilities. She was quizzed about her home life: did she have to take care of us? was she resentful? Were we a burden to her? Did she miss out on having a childhood? Sometimes the questions were implied; at other times they were quite direct.

Her answers always warmed my heart and brought tears to my eyes. She told them she had been taught from infancy to accept people of all colors, creeds, and disabilities. She told them about going along with her parents to conferences all over the country. She told them about meeting Ed Roberts when she was little, and, later, meeting Justin Dart. She reminded them that she participated in soccer and ballet and had even attended a Neil Diamond concert.

I contacted the school's psychology teacher once and tried to get Disability Simulation Day stopped. It was a lost cause. She liked having Disability Simulation Day featured in the local newspaper, and saw no need for me or my husband — or anyone from our local independent living center — to come to her classroom to talk with the students.

Every March, the Indiana Governor's Planning Council for People With Disabilities does a really stupendous job providing materials for people in celebration of Disability Awareness month. Their posters are excellent, as are their public service announcements.

But their "Disability Awareness Activities" booklet, one of their handouts, is horrendous. Here are a couple of excerpts from their publication. You decide:

All Thumbs (physical disabilities, group activity)

*Materials: masking tape, raisins, nuts, pudding.*

Activity: Sometimes people with physical disabilities don't have good muscle control. With masking tape, tape together the fingers of the participant's weaker hand, leaving only the thumb free. Give each participant a cup of raisins or a dish of pudding to eat using only that hand. Divide participants into pairs. Let one in each pair feed the other a dish of pudding. Trade places.

*Discussion: How did you feel during these experiments? Did you find ways to overcome the problems of eating when you had less control of your hands? How does it feel to be fed by someone else?*

"Thick Hands"

*Materials: thick socks, shirts, sweaters, shoes, beads, string and ruler.*

Activity: Some people have trouble with fine motor coordination. This is because their muscles are weaker, and they need more time and practice to learn how to move. To help participants understand this condition, have them put a pair of thick socks on each hand and try to tie shoes, button a shirt and string beads. Tie a ruler between the students' ankles so that their legs are stiff and apart from each other. Have them walk down the hall and back, slowly. How would they feel if people laughed or stared at them or imitated the way they walked?

*Discussion: Some people who have these kinds of difficulties have mental retardation. Their muscles are weaker and their coordination is poor. But not everyone with these difficulties has mental retardation. Discuss this assumption. Can you assume that someone who can't use his or her hands has mental retardation?"*

Because I have paralyzed arms, I never wear tie shoes, a simple fashion decision that compensates for my inability to tie shoes. There's nothing demeaning about it. There are many such things students could learn. The activities detailed above, though, cannot help but suggest helplessness. They evoke pity and disgust. The raisins and pudding dribble out of participants' mouths and get splattered across their clean faces. Being fed, they can't help but conclude, is a demeaning experience.

Even the exercises' titles are offensive. "All Thumbs" is a cliché — for clumsiness. Suggesting that someone who can't use their hands has mental retardation, even if made ostensibly to prove it wrong, seems to beg the question. Would it not be more instructive to show a physics video of Stephen Hawking?

On May 5, in Joliet, IL, Joliet Central High School journalism students, turned loose on a "Disabled for a day" article in the local newspaper, had this to say: "My muscles started to hurt from sitting all day... although I was in physical pain, the worst part as knowing that many people have to endure this pain on a daily basis for the rest of their lives."

And, "I briefly felt how it would feel to be wheelchair bound for life. I couldn't keep the tears in my eyes."

And, "People with mental disabilities don't comprehend and learn like others, but they're carefree. I would love to be carefree at times."

And, "Trembling and shaking, I took my first steps blind...I felt like I was in a small, dark room... At the end of the day, I took off the blindfold. I was so grateful because so many people do not have the option of taking off the blindfold."

These were the honest feelings the students got from participating in an Awareness Day. Is this the message we really want to send about living with a disability?

I am baffled as to why non-disabled people see a need to simulate a disability in order to understand our situation. Across our nation in February, we celebrate Black History Month. Is it necessary for people with white skin to paint their faces black to better understand this minority? Should heterosexuals be asked to experience homosexuality so we are not homophobic?

Should I expect to be able to teach someone how to drive a car, diaper and dress a baby and make the bed with their feet as I do? Am I amazing? No; I am just living my life.

We, the people who live with disabilities, we who have so long advocated for being treated as full members of society, must reclaim our dignity and say "No!" to simulations. I long for the day when disability simulations are dumped into the trash cans of oblivion.

**WHAT CAN BE DONE** to help the non-disabled masses understand the disability experience?

Talk to us and ask us questions. Ask persons who have had a disability from birth (or a long-time disability) to come to your class or organization.

Read publications written *by* persons with disabilities: Ragged Edge, Mouth magazine, Braille Monitor.

There are some really excellent books out there, too. Here are some of my favorites:

- ☛ **Reflections from a Different Journey What Adults with Disabilities Wish All Parents Knew,** by Stanley D. Klein & John D. Kemp

- ☛ **Make Them Go Away Clint Eastwood, Christopher Reeve & the Case**

**Against Disability Rights**, by Mary Johnson

☛ **Moving Violations: War Zones, Wheelchairs, and Declarations of Independence**, by John Hockenberry

☛ **By Trust Betrayed**, by Hugh Gregory Gallagher

☛ **FDR's Splendid Deception,** by Hugh Gregory Gallagher

☛ **Don't Laugh At Me**, by Steve Seskin and Allen Shamblin / Illustrations by Glin Dibley. Afterword by Peter Yarrow (ages 4-8)

☛ **No Pity,** by Joseph P. Shapiro

☛ **Awakening To Disability Nothing About Us Without Us**, by Karen G. Stone

☛ **Extraordinary People With Disabilities**, by Deborah Kent. Short essays profile 48 famous people — John Milton, Helen Keller, FDR, Tom Cruise — who have disabilities.

# Appendix F: Event Access Checklist

Be sure your Awareness Event is accessible! The place where you hold your event must be accessible. Use this checklist to find out what you need to do to be sure you are providing access.

## Accessible Entrance / Path of Travel

**Can people get to your event from the parking lot without going up steps or changes in level?**

___ Yes       ___ No? Then do the following:

> ☛ Add a ramp or lift.
>
> ☛ Point out a well-marked alternate route on level ground.

**Is there appropriate signage directing attendees to accessible entrances and bathroom facilities?**

___ Yes       ___ No? Then do the following:

> ☛ Post directional signage through accessible route.

**Is the path at least 36 inches wide?**

___ Yes       ___ No? Then do the following:

> ☛ Enlarge the pathway.
>
> ☛ Relocate event.

**Are curb cuts located in parking lot and at drop-off areas?**

___ Yes       ___ No? Then do the following:

> ☛ Install curb cut or add ramp to curb.
>
> ☛ Relocate event.

**Are sufficient numbers of accessible parking spaces available closest to the accessible entrance?**

___ Yes       ___ No? Then do the following:

> ☛ reconfigure spaces to provide accessible parking spaces (8 feet wide with an additional 5-foot access aisle) and lift-equipped van spaces (16 feet wide with 98 inches of vertical clearance).
>
> ☛ Relocate event.

## Usability of rest rooms

**Is there at least 1 fully accessible male and female rest room or 1 accessible unisex rest room?**

___ Yes       ___ No? Then do the following:

> ☛ Relocate event to be in proximity to accessible rest room.
>
> ☛ Reconfigure rest room or combine rest rooms to create a single unisex accessible rest room.

## Event room(s)

**If the site has multiple floors, is there an accessible elevator to the meeting room(s)?**

___ Yes      ___ No? Then do the following:

☛ Relocate event.

**Is an accessible path of travel available to the meeting room?**

___ Yes      ___ No? Then do the following:

☛ Relocate event.

**Is the meeting room accessible for speakers? Can participants navigate easily in the space?**

___ Yes      ___ No? Then do the following:

☛ If furniture is movable and seating is not tiered, reconfigure space. Otherwise, relocate event.

**Does your meeting space have windows or natural light sources (skylights)?**

___ Yes      ___ No? Then do the following:

☛ Make sure fluorescent lighting can be turned off, and incandescent lighting used, if needed. Otherwise, relocate event space for access to natural light (people with some kinds of neurological disabilities cannot function with fluorescent lighting.)

**Does your meeting space have an assistive listening system?**

___ Yes      ___ No? Then do the following:

☛ Obtain assistive listening system for meeting space, or locate to space that has access to one.

**Do you have a sign language interpreter or CART provider?**

___ Yes      ___ No? Then do the following:

☛ Hire interpreter or CART provider.

## Publicity/Invitations for Event

**Does your publicity/invitation contain information regarding access and availability of accommodations?**

___ Yes      ___ No? Then do the following:

☛ Add statement to publicity information that event will be accessible.

## Access to materials (See page 82.)